It is only upon the reading of David Moody's retelling of a near fatal car accident that almost ended his son's earthly life that one understands the title. Joshua was "rewired" and with him the author, his family, and a very close group of friends and new friends who journeyed together. They endured an experience everyone prays never happens to them or ones they love. There are other possible titles Mr. Moody could have used to describe the depth of faith, the power of prayer, the resilience of love, or the journey of those who accompanied the Moody family through a gripping and intensely emotional experience. David Moody keeps the reader wondering throughout if the "rewiring" would end in success. Not for any gratuitous effect, but rather as the story actually unfolded. For those who know the Moody family, their experience of the car accident and the resulting rewiring process was miraculous, but not surprising. It is a story of unyielding faith and the refusal to surrender to the odds of survival. It was also a young man's rewiring as so many good friends who were a part of a story while ever so patiently waiting for a happy ending that was never guaranteed. By book's end we are reassured that in the world of God and faith, hope springs eternal, something we should never forget.

—*Bishop Francis I. Malone, Diocese of Shreveport*

DAVID MOODY

THE
REWIRING
PROJECT

A story of faith, family
and extreme trauma

Jacksson David, LLC
North Little Rock, Arkansas

Published 2024 by Jacksson David, LLC, North Little Rock, Arkansas
First edition
Manufactured in the United States of America
ISBN 979-8-218-44149-4
Library of Congress Control Number: 2024917355
Editorial production by Liz Russell Solutions
Book design by Gloria C. White & Associates

At least half of the revenue from the purchase of this book (https://rewiringproject.com) will be donated to Miracles for Mary and Immaculate Conception School. Miracles for Mary is a nonprofit that has supported many TBI survivors and their families—including ours—over the years, following a horrific accident that left Jim and Patti Drake's daughter, Mary, with multiple serious injuries including a traumatic brain injury. The staff and students at Immaculate Conception School were wonderful to us! Prayers, food, chauffeur services, furniture rearranging, financial support and more. They are our family, and we love them.

Please access our website online at https://rewiringproject.com to buy the book directly from us so more money goes to our designated charities. With every purchase, the reader will receive a free link to an array of behind-the-scenes pictures, videos, posts. and hand-written notes that will make each chapter come alive as you read.

Dedication

This book is dedicated to folks past and future; to the countless family members, church and school family, friends, donors, CaringBridge responders, doctors, nurses, and medical staff who supported and inspired us on this miraculous journey; and to the many survivors of extreme trauma, their families, and caregivers. We hope this story gives you hope and strengthens your faith.

Acknowledgments

I must acknowledge my dear Gwen who endured rereading the details of this challenging journey despite having to reexperience the trauma again and again, and Liz Russell for her patience and guidance throughout the journey of publishing my first book.

Contents

The Crash 1

Settling in to Reality 11

Three A.M. 17

The Dark Days 21

A Vision and a Promise 29

Survive and Advance 33

Sorry, Sir, We Have to Ask You to Leave 55

Texas Bound 65

The Top of the Roller Coaster 69

The Fog Begins to Clear 89

The Whisper was a ROAR 105

Homecoming 131

Medical Biographies 143

The Crash

I couldn't move. The metal frame was wrapped around me like a glove. My hips were wedged into the seat, and my feet were trapped. Joshua lay beside me, unconstrained and unconscious. His head was on my right hip. His body was a bit twisted, and he was almost horizontal in the passenger's seat of his Toyota MR2. Motionless. Quiet. I could see him breathing, so I knew he was still alive. There were no obvious injuries. For a few seconds, I could hear the birds chirping and the wind blowing through the trees. It was strange how a few seconds of violence and noise could be followed so abruptly by such an eerie calm.

The silence was broken by a voice from behind me. "Are you okay?"

"No," I said.

"Do you need us to call 911?"

"Yes."

And so it began. What started as a fun drive in the park on a beautiful fall afternoon had turned into a struggle to survive. The journey that followed was scary, magnificent, humbling, and nothing short of miraculous.

It was the afternoon of Veteran's Day, Nov. 10, 2017. My son, Joshua, and I had decided to do something we had never done, take the afternoon off to enjoy a drive in his 2002 Toyota MR2. We have always been busy guys, and such opportunities rarely presented themselves. After years of running small businesses, startup tech companies, and a consulting business, I had recently accepted a position as the Deputy Director of the U.S. Small Business Administration's state district office. Joshua had been hard at it for several years after starting a tech company when he was seventeen and a junior in high school. Now twenty-one, he worked long hours on his business pursuits. Neither one of us was prone to taking time off.

When Joshua made enough money to buy his own car, he traded in the old Pontiac my wife, Gwen, and I had bought him for a 2002 Toyota MR2 Spyder convertible. It was all black, had a manual transmission and four-cylinder engine, and handled like a small sports car. Although the paint and interior were a bit worn and he had to rebuild the stereo, it was fun to drive; because they were difficult to find in good condition, he knew it would hold its value. Typical Joshua. Even when buying a fun thing, he was thinking about its future value.

I met Joshua at his apartment, and we got in the car. We decided to start off with lunch, and after a great meal and some good conversation, we hopped back in the car, put the top down, and headed to a local park. The park had been the location of many soccer practices and games in Joshua's younger years and included a beautiful tree-lined, winding paved road that fit our plans perfectly. Joshua was behind the wheel when we entered and drove all the way to the back of the park. Neither one of us had ever driven this road all the way to the back, so we decided to scout it out first at a slower speed before we started negotiating the turns and slight hills while working the gears at a higher speed.

When we had driven quite a distance on our scouting mission, we decided to turn around and drive back to the front of the park. Joshua drove first, working through the gears like a pro as he downshifted with perfect timing in the curves and used the straightaways to reach the reasonable maximum speed. I was impressed. He had developed into a skilled driver and clearly had a great feel for how his car handled.

Once we returned to the front of the park, we stopped, traded seats, and I began to drive. I had only driven Joshua's car short distances but had enough experience with manual transmissions to be comfortable in his car. I drove to the back of the park. It was great fun. There were a few places along the road where I had to downshift and brake to make a curve, and I also encountered another vehicle or two. The road we were driving led to the soccer fields near the entry of the park. Once I had finished my driving, we swapped seats again, and Joshua took another turn.

When it was my turn again, I jumped into the driver's seat with more confidence. We had taken three trips on the same road at this point, and I felt like I knew the road well enough to anticipate the turns and hills a bit better and negotiate them with a little more speed and efficiency.

I felt more comfortable on my second drive through the park. My braking and shifting were smoother, and I felt like I was in a better rhythm. Soon we came to the end of a short straightaway leading to a small hill high enough to block the view on the other side. As it turned out, a sharp left curve and an oncoming car awaited me. I topped the hill and was surprised to find the other car in the opposite lane. Rattled, I overcompensated to the right in an effort to make sure I stayed in my lane while negotiating the left-hand curve. Unfortunately, this back road had no paved shoulder, and trees lined the route just a few yards off the asphalt; it gave me no room for error. The paved road rose several inches above the ground, so turning back onto its surface at that angle would have been very difficult.

Had I had some open space just off the road, it's possible that I could have brought the car to a safe stop. But I had none. By overcompensating to the right and taking us off the pavement, I had inadvertently pointed the car directly at a large tree. Given our speed and lack of space to maneuver, I couldn't avoid it. In the same split second that I realized the tragic inevitability of our situation, a final thought came to my mind that gave me a sense of clarity and purpose. My only option at this point was to turn the car as far to the right as I could so that it hit the tree on my side instead of Joshua's.

So I did.

My recollection is that as soon as I turned the steering wheel, we made impact with the tree. Amazingly, I never lost consciousness. The impact was abrupt, violent, and destructive. The top was down, and my head was just a foot or so from the tree. The driver's side front quarter of the car was crushed, and as it turned out, I was as well. Immediately, I began assessing the situation. My first concern was Joshua. His head was on my hip and he wasn't moving or conscious. I checked his pulse and respiration—he was still alive. But I didn't feel like I could do anything to help him without freeing myself from my confinement. I quickly realized that I was wedged into my seat and that both my feet were trapped.

The left front portion of the car was a mangled mess of metal, plastic, and wires. The driver's side floorboard no longer existed. My door was still attached to the car but bent outward where it had wrapped around the tree. The windshield was shattered, and glass was everywhere. It appeared that our airbags had deployed although I don't actually remember that happening. My seat was twisted and crunched to about two-thirds its original size.

My initial assessment of the situation happened in seconds. As I was trying to figure out what to do next, I heard a voice from behind me ask if we were okay or needed help. It was the driver who had been traveling the opposite direction and had come to the curve in the road at the same time we did. They called the police on our behalf. Now that I knew that help was on the way, I refocused on what I could do to improve our situation.

I struggled to free my left foot, then my right. Neither came out. I tried again, with more effort. Nothing. After several very uncomfortable attempts, I realized that freeing my feet was going to be painful and require quite a bit of effort. I could feel them, so that was good. Unfortunately,

I couldn't see them, so I had no way of assessing whether I should even attempt to pull them out. My left foot seemed to be slightly more free, so I started with that one. After what seemed like an eternity, many tries, and some pain, I was able to free it as it came out of my shoe.

With my left foot freed, I attempted to reposition myself in the seat to gain more leverage to help free my right foot. When that didn't work, I decided to try to get my phone out of my pocket and call Gwen. I don't remember much about that call. I do remember my hands shaking, making it difficult to dial the number. She answered.

Gwen taught second grade at Immaculate Conception, our Catholic church school. When I called, she was in the library down the hallway from her classroom, preparing for their upcoming book fair. School had dismissed, but many of the teachers were still there. Gwen didn't have her phone with her in the library but when she returned to her room, it rang. Gwen said I sounded shaken as I informed her that we'd been in an accident. The first responders arrived as we spoke, and my status instantly changed from survivor to patient.

A policeman took the phone and finished the call with Gwen. He confirmed that we'd been in a bad accident.

"Are they okay, officer?" she asked.

"They are doing the best they can to take care of them, ma'am. Your son is unconscious, and they are taking him to UAMS. Is there someone who can drive you, ma'am?" he asked.

"Yes," Gwen replied.

"Your husband is going to UAMS as well, ma'am," he added. UAMS—the University of Arkansas for Medical Sciences—is a research hospital and medical school located in Little Rock's midtown.

Gwen thanked him and ended the call.

Before the call was even over, Gwen was headed to the front office. The school's vice-principal, Nicole Schafer, was in the hallway with a few other teachers and staff members. When she saw Gwen walking briskly down the hallway with a phone to her ear and a hand on her chest, she immediately knew something was wrong. Gwen delivered the news. Despite offers to drive her to the ER, Gwen insisted she drive herself. I suppose, at that moment, it was the only thing in her life she felt she could control. Maureen Berry, the office manager, joined her as Gwen hurried to her room to retrieve her things, not sure what to do first. "Get your purse and leave everything else," Maureen guided. This focused Gwen. She grabbed her purse, and off they went. Maureen asked again about driving, but Gwen was adamant. On the way, Maureen took a rosary from her purse, and they prayed together while Maureen reviewed the best route to the hospital with Gwen.

Back at school, teachers and staff members had begun praying for all of us.

Meanwhile, first responders were assessing our condition. It didn't take long for them to figure out that I was trapped and, despite having only minor cuts and lacerations, Joshua was seriously injured. As they checked him, he began to shake. He was alive but unconscious and seizing. Before they even attempted to move him, they needed to get me out of the way. That meant cutting me out of the car. They used cutting equipment to remove part of the steering wheel as well as the metal that trapped my right foot. Because I was not in pain, I had no way of knowing that the impact had crushed my pelvis.

The first responders helped me stand up; I was wobbly and weak but didn't think much about that given what had just happened. Once I stood up, things happened pretty quickly, and I lost track of Joshua as they were putting me on a gurney and into the ambulance.

EMTs and firemen were working quickly. The phone call must have lasted just long enough for the officer to tell Gwen we were being taken to UAMS. What I didn't understand at the time was that UAMS was the only Level 1 trauma center in the state and the only hospital that could give Joshua the care he needed.

Off we went.

Once in the ambulance, my thoughts focused on Gwen and Joshua. I had my phone with me. Since I had no living immediate family, I began to call my nephews and a few others to let them know what had happened and ask them to go to the hospital to support Gwen. Fortunately, they were dependable, family men of strong faith, and I knew I could count on them to do whatever it would take to help Gwen.

———◆———

I could see Gwen through the windows of the back door of the ambulance as we arrived at the University of Arkansas for Medical Sciences. At that moment, all I could think of was that her world had been turned upside down. I had no idea about the extent of my own injuries; all I knew was that the last time I had seen Joshua, he was unconscious and having a seizure at the scene of the accident. In a split second, Gwen went from the normal end of a school day to extreme fear and panic.

As they wheeled me in, she asked if I was okay and we held hands briefly. I responded that I was alright, although in that moment I had no idea, and urged her to stay with Joshua. We both said, "I love you" and went our separate ways.

I don't believe I have ever felt as lonely and out of control as I did in the first few hours at the hospital. In a matter of seconds, I went from the ambulance to an exam room surrounded by what seemed like at least a half dozen people. The lights were bright, I felt a bit groggy, and my instructions were to lie still so they could check me out. I never really knew how many folks were working on me; having seen too many hospital shows on TV, I assumed it was almost the entire ER staff.

For around fifteen minutes, I was in the eye of a hurricane of activity like I'd never experienced. Someone put an IV in me while others took off my clothes, poked me all over, and asked lots of questions. I wasn't always sure whether they were talking to each other or to me. Every few seconds, someone would come close to my end of the bed and ask me a direct question. My responses always seemed much slower than the speed of their questions. Then, as quickly as they came, they were gone. I never knew who they were, and I never got a chance to say thank you.

For what seemed like an eternity, I lay on the bed in the ER exam room. Periodically, someone would come in and do something to me or take something from the room. Eventually, Gwen came in. We kissed and held hands. She was being so strong for me. She hadn't seen Joshua yet but told me that several family members and friends were in the family waiting room with her, just outside the doors of the ICU. It was a short visit. Since I was stable, we both knew that she had to be with Joshua as soon as they moved him to a room. It was easy to see that she was torn. She wanted to stay with me but knew she couldn't. What an unbearable decision! Two of the three people she loved most in the world (we have two adult children) were in peril—one more than the other—and she had to choose.

Gwen left to return to the waiting room. That's when the loneliness of the situation began to set in. I was in the ER alone, unsure if I should try to move. In those moments, I had no idea where Joshua was or how he was doing, whether he was in pain or even still alive. I knew my wife was worried out of her mind. Not only had I caused this situation, I could do absolutely nothing about it.

I've always been the "fixer." The guy, at home or at work, who identifies the problem, figures out the options to solve it, makes a decision, and then executes. It just always came naturally to me. But now, I had no control, no viable options … and even if I did, I likely couldn't execute them. Though I knew the situation was temporary and that I'd eventually be reunited with my family, my mind couldn't keep from racing with unthinkable outcomes, pushing my patience to the limit.

With no control of the situation and no viable options, all I could do was talk to God.

Settling in to Reality

Joshua was rushed to the ER upon arrival at the hospital. According to the medical records, his initial diagnosis was a "closed head injury with loss of consciousness." He had a traumatic hemorrhage of the cerebrum, a laceration on his left eyebrow, and a traumatic pneumothorax (which we would learn is air in areas of the lung it's not supposed to be caused by trauma, with the potential of partial or total lung collapse).

The brain has three main parts: the cerebrum, cerebellum, and brain stem. The cerebrum is the largest part of the brain and is composed of right and left hemispheres. It performs higher functions—like interpreting touch, vision, and hearing—as well as speech, reasoning, emotions, learning, and fine control of movement. While we were focused on basic survival at this point, it was hard to think about Joshua without some or all of these functions.

Speculation was that the impact had thrown him into the steering wheel. I'm still baffled by this because we both were wearing seat belts—we always did. The EMTs put on a neck brace and gave him a dose of midazolam prior to arriving at the ER. Midazolam is a situational sedative that was likely administered to counter the seizure that Joshua experienced at the scene of the accident. Once in the ER, he received a CT scan and X-rays. Due to his unresponsive state, lung contusion, and hypoxia (deprivation of adequate oxygen supply), the decision was made to intubate (placement of a flexible plastic tube into the trachea to maintain an open airway or to serve as a conduit for drug administration). The medical team also started IVs of saline, Fentanyl for pain and sedation, and a few other stabilizing drugs. Finally, an external ventricular drain (EVD) was installed to monitor the pressure in his skull. In traumatic brain injury (TBI) patients, it's not unusual for the brain to swell in the first few days after trauma. If this happens, emergency procedures may be necessary to avoid additional damage to the brain as swelling causes it to push against the inside of the skull. The EVD had a sensor connected to a monitor at Joshua's bedside.

In the ER, Joshua was given a Glasgow Coma Score (GCS) of 3. The GCS assesses eye opening, verbal responses, and motor reflexes. Each of the three areas of the GCS has its own scale. The scales for eye opening and verbal responses run from 1 to 4 and 1 to 5, respectively. Joshua's score in both of these areas was 1. The scale for motor reflexes runs from 1 to 6. Joshua's score on this scale was 5 (Abnormal Flexion), which means that placing pressure in certain areas emitted a response of his arm bending at the elbow toward his chest.

A GCS of 3 overall is not good. Many studies involving thousands of patients ages five to seventy-five have provided significant insight into TBI survival rates and long-term outcomes. The odds of a good outcome with a GCS score of 3 ranges from 5 percent to 25 percent. Those percentages begin to improve a bit starting at a score of 5.

Joshua had several factors in his favor that increased his odds of survival and a good long-term outcome. He was young, his brain was still forming and more adaptable to change, and he was in good physical condition (although a bit underweight, according to his momma). As a young entrepreneur, he had a fairly high-functioning brain. Finally, he had no other serious injuries. Many times, TBI patients—especially those involved in motor vehicle accidents—have multiple injuries, many of them very serious. Treatment of all these injuries simultaneously can certainly complicate TBI recovery.

Until I started writing this book, I did no research into Joshua's odds of survival. For me, it didn't matter. Intuitively, I knew that the odds of a positive outcome or even survival were not good. But wallowing in negativity wasn't going to help this situation. It would only undermine the positive attitude I knew I needed to have—for Gwen, Joshua, and the medical staff. If they didn't believe in the possibility of a good outcome, it simply made matters worse. Honestly, at times I felt like I was hanging on by a thread, afraid that exposure to the stark reality and potential negative outcomes of this situation might pull me into the abyss. Was this our new reality?

Since all I could do for Joshua and Gwen was pray, I tried to focus my immediate attention on doing whatever it took to get me well enough to see them as soon as possible. The extent of my injuries was multiple lacerations on my ankles and lower calf, a sore left foot, and a broken pelvis. In this case, "broken" was shorthand for cracked in multiple places, pulled apart in others, and misaligned. Plus, there was some internal bleeding near my pelvis. When I got the diagnosis, all I could think of was that old, very insensitive joke: "Other than that, Mrs. Lincoln, how was the play?" It was what it was. There was nothing I could do but pray for the doctors treating me and for the strength to handle whatever came our way.

I fully expected to be in a great deal of pain—the kind you experience when you break multiple ribs and every movement hurts. I wasn't. The only explanation I have is that God knew we had a lot on our plate and spared me that burden. I can't imagine how difficult it would have been to help my family had I been in constant pain or on debilitating pain medication. As it turned out, the accident happened on a Friday afternoon, my surgery was Sunday morning, and by Thursday, Ashley, one of my regular nurses who quickly became a friend, was sneaking me to the ICU to visit Joshua.

Following my surgery I was moved to a room on the trauma floor and allowed to receive more visitors. It was great to be able to see Gwen more frequently, and she kept me updated on Joshua's condition. My nephews,

Micah and Greg, were there with Gwen on the day of the accident and dropped by every few days to check on me.

The entire medical staff did a great job of caring for me. Nurse Ashley endeared herself to us because she was always straightforward about what was going on and what to expect regarding my recovery and Joshua's condition. She gave me news that she knew I didn't want to hear, always pointed out the positive side of the situation, and consoled us when there wasn't a positive side. She knew that the pain I was dealing with was far more mental than physical. Sometimes she just listened. What a blessing she was.

For Gwen, the hours of not knowing were almost unbearable. Her sister Cindy Roberts was invaluable in those early hours and days after the accident. Gwen trusted her; Cindy is a "get 'er done" kind of person. She was consoling but wasn't afraid to ask questions, make decisions, or take charge if necessary.

It was good that Cindy was there; Gwen needed her. Her beloved son was on a ventilator, had multiple IVs, sensors all over his upper body, and a drain in his skull to relieve pressure. The IVs were connected to a host of medications from saline drips to heavy narcotics to keep him sedated and his heart rate, blood pressure, and temperature under control. The narcotics were administered through several digital pumps at Joshua's bedside. Sensors connected to monitors showed Joshua's vitals. These monitors became our up-to-the-minute data feed on how he was doing. The nurses could see those monitors from outside the room as well. It was a frightening and seemingly hopeless situation.

Three days after the accident, they lowered Joshua's sedation, and he was able to respond at times to commands with a thumbs-up, eye blinks, and other responses that let us know his brain was intact and that he could think and communicate. Though still sedated, the fact that he was responding at all was very positive and gave us hope.

As part of Joshua's initial treatment upon his arrival, the medical staff inserted a pressure sensor in his skull to monitor whether his brain was swelling. Swelling is not uncommon in severe TBIs. The problem is that if the brain begins to swell, it will quickly begin to press against the skull and cause even further brain damage. After four days, the sensor was removed because there had been no appreciable changes in pressure.

Around three o'clock on the morning of November 15—five days after the accident—Joshua began to show signs that something had gone horribly wrong.

Three A.M.

Three A.M. on Day Five, November 15, 2017. Alexis, Joshua's nurse that night, noticed readings indicating that his brain was beginning to swell. Without room to expand, his brain could begin to press against the inside of his skull and cause further brain damage or even death. She immediately notified Joshua's ICU doctor, who contacted the trauma surgeon on call. Joshua was rushed to emergency surgery.

Gwen called me, crying and emotional, around four that morning. She explained what was happening. My feelings of helplessness grew exponentially with that call. My wife was facing the prospect of our son on death's door, and I was unable to help and comfort her. They had wheeled Joshua to surgery, leaving Gwen alone in his room. Tears were flowing when the chaplain came in to offer help and comfort. Gwen thanked her but said she didn't want to see anyone at the moment. She had already called her sister Cindy, who was on the way.

Dr. Analiz Rodriguez was the trauma surgeon on call that early morning. She had just returned from being off work for a few days and was placed on the on-call schedule.

Dr. Rodriguez is the Director of Neurosurgical Oncology at UAMS and has an independent brain tumor research laboratory in the Winthrop P. Rockefeller Cancer Institute. A young but accomplished neurosurgeon, she had been at UAMS only a few months before the accident. She is very close with her mother, who had moved with her to Little Rock in the summer. With her background, Dr. Rodriguez had many interviews and opportunities. She chose UAMS because she had the opportunity to launch a brain tumor program and because of her desire to improve health disparities in the southern U.S.

Dr. Rodriguez had been informed of Joshua's arrival in the ER five days earlier due to his brain injury. She had seen his original CT scans showing significant bruising in the front of his brain on both sides. As fate would have it, she was the surgeon on call that early morning to take the urgent case from the trauma team.

To Dr. Rodriguez, there was nothing out of the ordinary about Joshua's surgery. We would come to love her calm, confident demeanor. It's hard to imagine her wielding a very sharp knife and power tools, but those are the tools of a brain surgeon. The craniectomy involves shaving the patient's head, at least partially, and making an incision in the outer layer of skin so the surgeon can pull it back and expose the portion of the skull that needs to be removed. In Joshua's case, both sides of his brain were damaged and swelling, so Dr. Rodriguez made an incision from ear to ear across the top of his head. Once the skin was pulled back, she used special cutting tools to remove portions of his skull in the front on both sides of his forehead. Those skull sections, referred to as skull flaps, were collected and stored in a sterile environment so they could be reinstalled at a later date (often months later) once the swelling subsided. With the skull flaps removed, Dr. Rodriguez could cut through the durma, the thin layer of protective material that covers the brain. Once the pressure on his brain was relieved, Joshua was stitched up and sent to recovery.

When Dr. Rodriguez came into Joshua's room after surgery, she found Gwen on the edge of his bed. She appeared to be praying. The doctor noticed prayer cards and other religious items scattered around the room. By this time, Gwen had been living in the ICU for five days, so it was not surprising that she had surrounded herself with items from home that gave her comfort. Dr. Rodriguez briefed Gwen on the surgery, and they talked a bit. She asked Gwen if she'd like to pray with her.

It turned out that Dr. Rodriguez was also Catholic. She and her mother had a strong Catholic faith and a devotion to Mary, as do many Catholics, based on Mary's special place in the church. Displays of faith and religion, however, are not so common in hospitals or with surgeons; in fact, they are against policy in some institutions. Fortunately, when Dr. Rodriguez was in medical school, she met a doctor who was a faith-based person. "He said he routinely wore something that indicated he was open to prayer," she recalls. "So later in training I began to wear an angel pin as a demonstration of my faith and openness to prayer. I didn't want to offend anyone, but sometimes people would ask me to pray with them. In recent years, I've begun to ask when I see indications that it's okay."

Of all the surgeons who could have been on call that early morning, Joshua's surgery was performed by a highly skilled, compassionate, faith-filled doctor who shared our Catholic beliefs and was open enough with her faith to invite Gwen to pray the first time they met. It was exactly what Gwen needed in that moment of despair. God gives us what we need when we need it.

We believe that nurse Alexis and Dr. Rodriguez saved Joshua's life that early morning.

The Dark Days

Joshua survived the emergency surgery. *Survive* is about the only term one can use to describe the result. We were thankful he was still alive, but we had no idea whether the swelling in his brain had caused any further damage. Joshua was heavily sedated. Now, we would wait and pray.

The first four or five days after Joshua's double craniectomy were what I refer to as the Dark Days. These days had a general feeling of helplessness and anxiety. We didn't know what to expect or how to prepare for it. We asked lots of questions and had many more rolling around in our heads. Most of them were unanswerable or unanswered. Dr. Rodriguez was away from the hospital during this time, so we couldn't talk with her. We were adrift in a stormy sea … at night … enveloped in darkness.

As soon as I was coherent after my own surgery, the first thing I asked for was to see Joshua. This intensified the day after Joshua's craniectomy. I didn't want ice chips or pain meds or a blanket, I wanted to see my son and wife. Given my prognosis and hospital policy, Nurse Ashley knew this could not be accomplished without some level of covert activity. I was confined to my room and in a minimal form of traction. She accepted the challenge.

Ashley, Nurse Ashley, or David's Nurse, as she came to be known, was my nurse for much of the time from my arrival at the hospital until my release. She was highly skilled, matter of fact, caring, and had a good sense of humor. During my stay, she went the extra mile to answer my many questions and listen intently, even when my emotions got the best of me during our conversation about the accident. She used the "underground nurses network" to keep me updated on Joshua in between visits from Gwen and my family members.

Since I was confined to my bed, the first plan was to find some pretext for transporting me within the hospital. The idea was that Ashley would simply wheel me, in my bed, down to Joshua's room, several corridors away but on the same floor. A bold move. I liked it. Who would dare question such a conspicuous act? Unfortunately, there were multiple challenges with this idea. First, transportation in a hospital is a big deal, typically requiring an order from a doctor or charge nurse to have the transportation staff come and move you. Second, for Ashley to vacate her duty station for a prolonged period violated several hospital policies and protocols. Not to mention the challenge of wheeling a bed, with a 220-pound patient in it, halfway across the hospital by herself. This requires a skill set akin to those of tugboat pilots and aircraft carrier captains. As the E-Trade commercial states, this sort of behavior was "frowned upon in this establishment." Other than that, it was a great idea.

A wheelchair was our only choice—faster, easier to maneuver, and less conspicuous. It is the motorcycle of the hospital fleet. The problem was that I wasn't cleared to leave the bed and wasn't sure I could, even if I tried. The only way to find out was to give it a shot. To this day, I'm not sure what Nurse Ashley did to spring me. All I know is that one day she came in my room with a wheelchair and a big smile on her face.

"Get in," she said. "We're going to see Joshua." She helped me into the chair, which gave me some slight discomfort but no pain.

It still amazes me to think about what a blessing that was. Thanks to Nurse Ashley, I was going to see Joshua for the first time since the accident. I was excited and scared at the same time. Just a day earlier, Joshua had undergone emergency surgery. I wasn't sure what condition he—or Gwen—would be in. I did know that it would be emotional and that I needed to stay strong. My heart ached for them. I was praying all the way down the hallway that God would give me what I needed to stay strong for both of them. I was trying hard to take deep breaths and control my emotions.

Some of the nurses on the floor seemed to know who I was and why I was there. They smiled as I passed them. I suspect Ashley had something to do with that. As I entered the room, I hugged Gwen, and we took a few minutes to console one another. I then went immediately to Joshua's bedside.

He was unconscious, immobile, and breathing through a tube. Bags of medications hung from the metal stands beside his bed, and tubes and wires were running everywhere. He wore what looked like a thin toboggan hat that covered the fifty-plus new stitches that ran from ear to ear across the top of his head. His head was covered from just above his eyebrows, around to the midpoint of his ears, and almost to his hairline in the back. His head was shaved from his hairline in the front to approximately the crown of his head. The surgery had not required his head to be shaved all over, but we would take care of that a few days later when one of the nurses, at Gwen's persistent request, knowing it was what he would want, agreed to shave the rest of his head.

I hadn't seen him since the accident. I was glad he was still with us. I couldn't see much of his handsome face due to the myriad of wires and tubes. Because I was in a wheelchair and unable to stand, I could only reach his arm and hand on one side as he lay in the bed. His eyes were closed. I spent quite a while holding his hand and talking to him. I wasn't sure he could comprehend my words, but it didn't keep me from reassuring him—and myself as well—that he was going to be okay, that we had lots of folks praying for him, and that God was with us. At that point, I was trying to convince myself as much as trying to sell him on that idea.

I was doing all I could to focus on being in the moment with Joshua and not on the fact that he was being kept alive by all these medications, tubes, IV lines, and machines. I was smiling on the outside but crying on the inside.

Shortly after my first visit with Joshua, I was discharged from the hospital. The reality was that I was going to be wheeled to another wing on the same floor and take up residence in Joshua's room with Gwen. My marching orders from the surgeon were to stay in the wheelchair, not stand up for any reason, and come back for a checkup in six weeks.

It didn't take us long to figure out that we could not keep everyone posted on Joshua's condition with texts and phone calls. We quickly experienced communication overload. Cindy, Gwen's sister, introduced us to the CaringBridge platform and set up an account for us. CaringBridge gives patients, and their caregivers, a means to communicate with friends and family, much like a message board. I began writing posts every few days on Joshua's condition. Friends and family could access the account 24/7 and leave comments if they wished.

Some of these posts are scattered throughout this book. They are essentially our diary entries and some selected comments from folks who followed us on the platform. They appear here—unedited, poor grammar, misspellings, warts, and all. When I responded to comments, those entries appeared with Joshua's name beside them. He definitely was not the person responding. Our very first post was on November, 21, 2017, eleven days after the accident and a week after his emergency craniectomy.

Our First Entry

November 21, 2017: In the first three days Joshua showed good early signs by responding to commands to wiggle his toes, give a thumbs up, hold up the correct number of fingers, and open his eyes. On November 15,

Joshua's brain began to swell rapidly and an emergency craniectomy, the removal of portions of his skull, was performed to give his brain room to swell. After the surgery, controlling his body's temperature became a challenge. Doctor's tell us that this is not unusual with a traumatic brain injury. For several days it was a constant balancing act between sedation and temperature. The sedation slowed his body down, and limited shivering and shaking which caused his temperature to rise, but also significantly limited his cognitive response. His temperature fluctuated between 101 and 103 F and he spent almost an entire day under cold blankets with ice bags under his arms and around his neck. Temperatures that spike frequently, or are sustained in this range, can caused further injury to the brain or death.

Most recently, a change in medicine has given him better temperature control. His temperature is still consistently above normal but not fluctuating into higher, more dangerous ranges. He is also getting some breathing treatments to keep his lungs clear. We are anticipating doing a tracheotomy today to help with breathing and limit his risk of lung issues caused from prolonged use of the intubation tube currently in use.

Doctor Rodriguez, the doctor that performed his craniectomy, has been away since his surgery but returned today. Gwen is very impressed with her. The doctor spent a great deal of time with Gwen this morning and prayed with Gwen at Joshua's bedside. Turns out she is also Catholic. Of all the doctors who could have been on call on November 15 at 3 A.M. God gives us what we need, when we need it.

Miracle in progress.

Clinically, Joshua had suffered significant damage to key parts of his brain. As is common with traumatic brain injury, this caused "storming." Storming, medically labeled as Paroxysmal Sympathetic Hyperactivity (PSH), occurs when your brain can no longer regulate key bodily functions such as temperature, blood pressure, and heart rate. It is a nervous system disorder that affects fifteen to thirty-three percent of people who have sustained a severe TBI. Onset of symptoms can occur within hours or months of the injury, and for family members with little medical background, the signs can be alarming: rapid breathing, sweating, agitation, abnormal posturing, elevated heart rate, blood pressure, and temperature are just a few.

For the first three weeks of Joshua's stay, temperatures of 103 F, a heart rate of 140, and erratic blood pressure were common on a daily basis. It was not unusual for his temperature and heart rate to be high for hours at a time, multiple times during the day. He was treated with sedatives and other medications to help regulate those functions. These medications had to be regulated very closely because his temperature, blood pressure, and heart rate could fall as quickly as they rose, creating a whole different set of life-threatening conditions requiring a different set of drug therapies.

Although Joshua was lying in a bed 24/7, his body was chewing through calories while his brain was working to recover, and his system was going through these frequent storming episodes. Despite being tube fed what were calculated to be sufficient calories to maintain his weight, Joshua would eventually lose approximately thirty pounds in thirty days—and virtually all of the muscle from his once-athletic body—and leave UAMS with a weight of only 132 pounds on his nearly 6'4" frame. He was under covers almost all the time, but when he was rolled over to change his sheets or perform some procedure, his hipbones and ribs were prominent. He looked nothing like the gifted soccer and basketball athlete of his teen years. Gwen could hardly bear to see it.

Gwen was in mourning. She felt she had lost her son. To see this vibrant, intelligent young man lying unresponsive in a hospital bed was almost more than she could take. This had shaken her to the core, and she was in a pretty dark place. Gwen's faith has always been strong, but this situation made her feel hopeless.

As if storming and loss of brain function were not enough, Joshua also had a breathing tube and received breathing treatments multiple times per day. Due to concerns about blood clots from his lack of activity, X-rays of his lungs were taken daily. We may not know for decades the impact of all the exposure to radiation.

In addition, the physical therapy team made braces for his feet and hands to help keep his limbs from curling into a disfigured position, a condition known as posturing. We changed these out several times a day while he was in the hospital. We hated the hand braces because it impaired out ability to hold his hand. We did a lot of hand holding and talking, even though he wasn't responsive. It also made it difficult to keep one of several crosses in his hands.

Our adult daughter, Emily, lives in northwest Arkansas, raising our young grandsons on her own. Living three and a half hours away, we don't see them as often as we'd like as it is. The situation was about to become even more challenging. Her ability to travel was limited, Gwen and I were about to have to focus on Joshua, and I was expected to be immobile for several months. The prospect of being isolated from her and her boys was daunting.

Our world, as we knew it, was in a dark place. We needed some sign of hope, and I was about to get it.

A Vision and a Promise

Despite this desperate situation, divine intervention gave me a different vision. My vision was that Joshua and God were working on the greatest rewiring project of all time.

From a very young age, Joshua was able to figure things out. At eight years old, he was taking apart the Happy Meal toys from McDonald's to see how they worked. On a number of occasions, I'd seen him take a bundle of wires connected to various pieces of nonfunctioning electronic equipment, sort it all out, repair what needed to be repaired, and make it all work. A bundle of wires that looked like a bowl of spaghetti would end up organized, labeled, and elegant.

I'll never forget the day that I realized that Joshua had a gift. He had an electronics project spread out on his mom's kitchen counter. Gwen did not like it when he did this, but he claimed the lighting was better and he had more room to spread things out ... and spread them out he did. As with most of his electronics projects, this one required dozens of parts and pieces, a magnifying glass, a printed circuit board, a variety of tools, and a soldering iron. Momma did not like it when he soldered on her kitchen counter. She always made him put a cookie sheet under his project in case the hot solder missed its intended target. Joshua seldom asked permission to work at the counter and almost never remembered the cookie sheet. This usually resulted in a brief scolding from Momma as she handed him the sheet to put under his project.

The cookie sheet served another purpose as well. If Joshua didn't finish his project before meal time, he was required to put all his parts, tools, and equipment on the cookie sheet and get it off the counter. As I recall, he always complained about this inefficient way of doing things, similar to the argument against making his bed every morning since he was going to get right back in it later that day. Joshua was always stating his case like a seasoned trial lawyer, but he was no match for his very worthy opponent. The moment that Gwen invoked both his first and middle names—"Joshua David," she'd say with her voice raised a bit—he knew it was over. He'd lower his head, pack his stuff, and retreat to his room.

On this particular day, I walked by the kitchen counter where Joshua was working. I stopped and observed him as he soldered some wires to complete an electrical connection. I asked a few questions about what he was working on. Joshua was looking through his magnifying glass, laser-focused on soldering. Suddenly, he stopped, looked up at me, and said, "Dad, I don't understand how I know how to do some of these things. I just do." At that moment, I knew that he was discovering his gifts and, just as important, that he understood them to be gifts he was born with.

As he lay in the hospital, I visualized Joshua untangling the mess of wires and circuitry in his brain just as he had with so many projects he had worked on, with Jesus standing beside him guiding his hands, reassuring him, and helping him to be patient and resilient. That gave me comfort that Joshua would be okay at some point. I didn't know what "okay" meant, and I didn't know when "at some point" would be; I just knew in my heart that it would happen. I had a strong feeling that, for whatever reason, God had His healing hand on all of us. Feeling that Joshua would be okay eventually, knowing that these nurses and doctors were working hard to keep him alive—and that they seldom knew if patients fully recovered once they left the ICU, as they had told us—I began to make a promise to the doctors and nurses that cared for Joshua.

The promise was simply this: "Joshua and I will walk back in here someday and give you all a proper hug." That was a bold statement for a guy in a wheelchair speaking for himself and his son, who was unconscious and immobile.

Survive and Advance

I began to feel optimistic about Joshua's recovery. I'm generally an optimistic person, but anyone would have had to dig pretty deep to see hope in this situation. I started researching TBI and quickly decided that knowing the statistics for survival and outcomes was only going to dampen my ability to be optimistic and support Gwen. Completely against my nature as a data guy, I chose to ignore the statistics. As far as I was concerned, this was in God's hands, and I trusted that He would guide the medical staff and give us the strength we needed to deal with whatever came our way, as long as we continued to pray and trust in Him. Our goal at this stage was to survive and advance

We needed a miracle, and there is only one way that can happen.

The ICU became our new home. We were at UAMS 24/7 with the rare exception when Gwen or I might stay at home overnight to get a full night's sleep and recharge just a bit. A number of people volunteered to stay the night with Joshua while we both went home, but we only did that twice. We couldn't bear leaving Joshua. Additionally, I was in a wheelchair during that time, and both of us being home just meant that Gwen had to help me get around. She worried about me more at home than in the hospital.

Hospital rules allowed only one person to stay in the room. Most of the nurses were understanding enough to allow us both to stay in the room most nights. When this didn't work out, I slept in the family room outside of the ICU. The family room had a dining and meeting area, refrigerator, bathroom with a shower, microwave, and a large bank of reclining chairs where family members could sleep. The room was lined with windows with a nice view from several floors up. Unfortunately, I never got to enjoy it since I waited as late as I could to leave Joshua's room and had to be up early to re-enter the ICU floor before access started being controlled around six-thirty.

It was a pretty lonely feeling to go into the family room late at night, in the dark, and prepare to sleep in a room full of folks I didn't know. Well, I didn't know them personally, but I knew that if they were in that room with me, the life of someone they loved was in danger. So there I was, in my wheelchair, in the dark, trying to be quiet, with my overnight bag that included a few toiletry articles, a clean shirt for the next day, my phone, and my urine bottle—sometimes referred to as my pee cup.

Gwen would get up early each morning and open the ICU door for me, and one of us would find some coffee to start the day. As little sleep as I got in the family room, it was still more sleep than Gwen got in Joshua's room. The nurses needed a reasonable amount of light to do their jobs, and someone came in every hour or so to check on him. In time, we would grow accustomed to the rhythms of the nursing floor and even joke about the interruptions.

Joshua was at UAMS for thirty-two days. We lived in his room whether he was in ICU or on the trauma floor. We got used to taking spit baths, as my mom used to say, where we quickly washed off as best we could in a bathroom sink. The doctors typically made their first rounds about seven. There were times when, having taken the equivalent of five one-hour naps during the night, we would simply rise up from our sofa bed to greet them and discuss Joshua's medical issues. Now I know how med students feel when doing their residencies. I think we may have startled some of the doctors who found us in Joshua's room at that hour of the morning. We were in survival mode and, quite honestly, far less concerned than we would normally be about our appearance or what anyone thought of us.

While I was working to stay positive and hopeful, Gwen was in mourning. The few times over the first month that Gwen left the hospital, she didn't want to come back. If she returned to our house, a part of her didn't want to leave the comfort and familiarity of home to return to the hopeless and stressful environment of the hospital.

A week or so after Joshua's surgery to remove his skull flaps, a resident came into his room. In the course of the conversation, she informed Gwen that he would never be the son she once knew. This was very upsetting to Gwen. We informed Dr. Rodriguez of the conversation. Not long after, the resident came to apologize to us. I was able to visit with her afterward, give her some of our back story, and share our strong belief that Joshua would recover. She was very receptive. I told her she was going to be a great doctor one day and I hoped this engagement made her an even better one.

Although I did what I could to comfort her with hugs and a positive attitude, I knew that Gwen would have to work through this on her own. She has always been a strong-willed woman. I prayed that God would help her see that Joshua being alive was a good thing and that there was hope for a good outcome.

At this point Gwen and I had been married for more than three decades, and there is no one I'd rather have by my side in a desperate situation—especially if the situation involved our kids. Let's just say that "Momma Bear" is an appropriate description. Like many of the mothers I know—including our daughter, Emily—anything that endangers the people she loves will invoke a level of ferocity and singular focus that is seemingly contrary to her kind and mild-mannered nature. I told Gwen that years ago I had observed a pattern in her response to challenging situations like this. Her initial reaction is typically panic, desperation, and negative thoughts. Once she gets that out of her system, she embraces the reality of the situation and begins to focus on solutions with a "lead, follow, or get out of the way" attitude. I usually just got out of the way or followed. Leading is not an option, as that slot is already taken. My mission, in the days immediately following the accident, was to help her work through her natural feelings of loss and desperation in the early stages of this situation so that she could transition into Momma Bear mode.

I saw some signs of this transition around Day Eight in the hospital, when Gwen had taken all she could of strange people showing up in Joshua's room to poke him or give him some medicine without announcing who they were, why they were there, or what they were doing to her son. While Gwen was still very emotional and in mourning, this gave her some sense of control in a situation where we had very little. As one of my old football coaches used to say to get us fired up for a game, "It was time to kick ass and take names."

And that she did. No one, and I mean no one—from housekeeping to the hospital administrator—entered Joshua's room without Gwen subjecting them to some form of interrogation. It didn't take long for the staff to catch on, and henceforth the folks who came to Joshua's room more than once stated their name and intentions as soon as they walked in.

She also began to display pictures of Joshua. Gwen was determined that anyone who came in our room saw that this was not just another patient, but her beautiful, accomplished son. She made it personal for the nurses and doctors. Since we were essentially living in Joshua's room, she started making it more like home with her favorite fragrances, low lighting, and religious items. One nurse commented that she enjoyed coming into our room because "It smells so good, and it's so peaceful."

We began to speak openly with the medical staff about Joshua, his life before the accident, and our faith. This prompted doctors and nurses to engage us in conversation about their lives and, on occasion, their faith.

Gwen also began to question certain protocols, what each medication did, and why the doctor had prescribed it. Our family has experienced this for years, sometimes rolling our eyes, as she thoughtfully interrogates doctors, pharmacists, online customer service people, and wait staff in restaurants.

Soon she knew every treatment and medication Joshua was on (there were a dozen at one point), what it did, how it affected him, and when he was supposed to take it. After a while, the nurses and doctors became confident that Gwen, because of her constant observation, was very knowledgeable about treatment options and how they affected Joshua. The staff began to listen to her suggestions and would even ask her what she thought regarding the dosage or timing of medications when there was some room for judgment. They even followed her advice when she recommended not giving Joshua a treatment or medication due to his current status and her observations from previous treatments.

After a couple of weeks in the ICU, we were advised by the medical staff to switch Joshua from the breathing tube down his throat connected to a respirator to a trach tube. A trach tube is a plastic tube inserted into the trachea through an incision in the throat. It allows the patient to breath on their own and can be fitted with a valve that allows the patient to speak. Our understanding was that keeping him on the breathing tube created greater long-term risk of infection and other complications associated with having a foreign object running down his throat and into his lungs. We were hopeful that moving from the breathing tube to the trach tube would help Joshua progress to breathing completely on his own again and eventually speaking.

When Thanksgiving was just two days away, our Immaculate Conception School family decided to surprise us and bring food to our house. It was a wonderful gesture. When anyone was facing difficulty, the IC School teachers and staff would routinely cook, bring food, run errands, and pitch in however needed. In this case, there were two challenges. One, we were at the hospital with Joshua. Two, we had a home alarm system.

Imagine the principal, vice-principal, staffers, and several teachers breaking into our home. When the alarm went off, someone was calling the police to confess, a few were searching for our cat, who quickly went into hiding, and others were trying to figure out how to get out of the house and disable the alarm. Keystone cops come to mind!

We needed to be with Joshua, who had been moved back to ICU for observation. We weren't coming home for Thanksgiving. So our school family brought Thanksgiving to us in the hospital. For the first time ever, Gwen and I were spending Thanksgiving away from family. Instead, we had our dinner in the UAMS ICU family room kitchen. It was a lonely feeling, and yet we felt blessed to be able to spend this Thanksgiving with Joshua, not at his funeral.

Thankful

November 22, 2017: Just wanted to say thank you for all the love and support. We have been very engaged with Joshua's care today. Good day as far as we are concerned because of the potentially bad news that we didn't get. Joshua's MRI, while still inconclusive in some areas due to swelling and other factors, did not show any major areas of the brain that were damaged beyond the bruising that we were already aware of. This will be a long, hard journey with many ups and downs over months and even years. However, with good therapy, hard work, the love and support of our friends and family, and the loving embrace and healing hand of God, we believe the prospects for a meaningful recovery are good.

We have a great challenge ahead but we have much

to be thankful for. Happy Thanksgiving everyone!! May God bless you all in abundance.

Trach day

November 24, 2017: Big day today. Doing a tracheotomy to get Joshua off the breathing tube. Will make him more comfortable and lower the risk of infection due to long term use of a breathing tube. We hope he will be breathing on his own soon and that they will be able to take out the trach tube in the not too distant future as well. As always, please pray with us for God's healing hand, for the doctors and nurses, and for the strength and patience to handle whatever comes. God is good, all the time. More later …

Post Trach

November 24, 2017: Completed trach an hour or so ago. Nurses tell us procedure went well. Haven't seen docs yet. We can see Joshua's entire handsome face now without all the breathing and feeding tubes around his face. Beautiful!! It will be a while before the sedation and pain meds wear off. Major step. One day at a time.

As it turned out, getting Joshua off the trach permanently would take far longer than we ever imagined.

Face Time

November 25, 2017: It sure is good to see Joshua's handsome face. Although, he will not like his new haircut when he becomes aware of it. The next few days will be focused on backing off his sedation and respiratory support and assessing him. That has already started this morning. While learning just how far Joshua has to go to recover will be daunting, we are excited to get the journey started. We will need every ounce of love, prayers and support that you all can muster. That, along with God's abundant love and healing hand will serve as our fuel for the journey. Thank you all in advance.

Sunday morning full of hope

November 26, 2017: A night of higher temps and other vitals followed by a TWO FINGERS sign when asked by a young resident. Only did it once and it could have been accidental since he was moving his hands around at the time, but we will take it. Today and the next few days are all about taking him off sedation and making sure he can tolerate the trach. These goals are required to move him out of ICU and into a unit that will provide a more normal level of care. This is both exciting and scary for us as his nurses will now have 4–5 other patients and not just him and one other.

We are most thankful for all the well wishes, visits, prayers and offers to help. I plan to use this website to post some opportunities that folks can volunteer for in the next few weeks. It is very difficult for us to ask for help, but we know we cannot do this alone. We are surrounded by friends and family who are sincere in their offers to help and we haven't done a very good job of telling them what we need, we don't know ourselves most of the time, and making it easy for them to help. I promise that we will do a better job of that going forward.

Finally, some of our friends are working on a Go-Fund-Me site to help us raise money for our mounting and long-term medical expenses. Many have already given us hundreds of dollars and we are most thankful for that. Our intent is to open a medical expense checking account with a local bank to help us account for donations and expenses. Again, asking for donations is not something we will do well but we know we will need it. We are most thankful and grateful for those who have already given and hope that, for those who would like to donate, we can make it easy for you to do so.

Doctors coming in. Enjoy this beautiful Sunday. It is the day the Lord has made. Let us rejoice and be glad.

It was gratifying to read responses such as this one:

Joshua, you have stalkers all over the country. You and your Dad are beloved far and wide. Praying for healing for you and wisdom for your medical team.

—*Sarah Daigle*

A few weeks after the accident, someone suggested that one of us consider becoming Joshua's guardian in order to legally make decisions on his behalf. Gwen and I struggled with the whole concept of having to do that for our son, possibly for the remainder of his life. It was a sobering thought and something with which no parent wants to be confronted. Yet, it was a reality and we had to deal with it.

Fortunately for us, we go to church with some trustworthy lawyers who have done this sort of work. Jim Hamilton, a retired judge and a member of my Men of Faith group, volunteered to help us free of charge. He guided us through the process with patience and care. We decided to make Gwen the legal guardian because she would be the primary caregiver and accompany Joshua to rehab while I returned to my job.

As a practical matter, the first order of business was to decide whether to keep Joshua's apartment. He earned enough money to afford a nice one-bedroom apartment in a nice part of town. From a medical standpoint, it was unclear whether he would ever recover enough to be able to live on his own at all, let alone in this particular third-floor apartment. Should we contact the apartment management to cancel the contract? Would they let him out without a substantial financial penalty? Should we hold on to the apartment for a few more months at least to see if he improved? If so, how would we handle the financial burden of paying his rent and utilities? The best decision was not clear. We didn't have good data or solid evidence to help us decide, but we had faith that Joshua would recover. We decided to keep the apartment and felt a way to pay for it would materialize at some point.

It was one thing to wonder privately whether Joshua would recover, it was quite another to publicly claim, in writing, his inability to care for himself and to take on that responsibility. It weighed heavily on Gwen. The process of filing for guardianship caused her to confront the reality that, for the foreseeable future, she would be responsible for every element of Joshua's life. Although we made these decisions together when we could, she could easily find herself in a situation in which she was the sole decision maker.

Drinkin' From a Firehose

November 30, 2017: I know the readers of these posts don't expect it, but I feel the need to apologize for not posting more frequently. I do the best I can to keep everyone up to date but there will be times on this journey, and the last few days have been an example of those times, when we are drinking from a firehose and there just isn't enough energy left to write a post. Sorry about that.

Where to start? The big, good news is that Joshua is now out of ICU and in a regular bed on the trauma floor (aka The Floor). 19 days in ICU. I must say, while we are appreciative of being medically stable enough to leave, we loved the care we received in the ICU and the doctors and nurses that provided it. What a blessing they have been. I pray that they each receive many blessings for the care they provided our Joshua. The move to The Floor was a clandestine operation carried out, in typical hospital fashion, in the dead of night. We are adjusting to our new floor medical family, and we like what we have experienced so far. Thanks to Nurse Ashley, my nurse when I was on this floor after my surgery, the transition has been easy. The plan is to not be here too long. More on that later.

Joshua is opening his eyes more often, tracking our movements, squeezing hands, giving a thumbs up, etc. Now that speech therapy has started, we are also seeing Joshua respond to stimuli and get closer to breathing normally without the trach. Small improvements, but that's how this sort of thing goes. By the way, the title of Speech Therapist is a very limiting description for what these professionals do. Their therapies include cognitive therapy and much more. Also, physical and occupational therapy will begin soon, and we are excited and anxious to see how Joshua responds to those therapies as well. Therapy needs to take place when he is alert and Joshua still sleeps quite a bit as his brain continues to heal. Rewiring takes a lot of energy.

We are already considering options for long term therapy. Some are in central AR and others are out of state. An important, and daunting decision. We have no idea when all that will take place. It depends on the pace of Joshua's progress to some degree. The Go Fund Me page is progressing thanks to Jeannette and Dottie we have set up a donation account with First Security Bank. More on this later. Thanks so much for all the thoughts and prayers. Keep 'em comin'. We need and feel each one.

It was strange how this tragic event brought us back together with some of our old friends. Families we were close to when our kids were younger and playing sports or going to school together seemed to come out of the woodwork and rally around us. Our kids had all grown up, gone their separate ways, and weren't very connected anymore other than occasionally on social media. Yet the bonds forged among the parents when our kids were in elementary, middle, and high school had stood the test of time. The Reeds, Niguses, Wendels, and Catheys were all there for us in a big way. Holding our hands, crying and praying, and questioning doctors and nurses with us. Staying the night with Joshua while we went home to rest. Bringing us food, clothes, and whatever else we needed. Giving us money, sometimes anonymously and in large amounts. What a tremendous blessing they all were. I hope we never have any need to return those favors in similar circumstances, but if we can, we will. What a blessing they all have been.

One day some of Joshua's friends came to visit, friends he had known since kindergarten. Seth went to Catholic High with Joshua, and Hannah and Jaci went to Mount Saint Mary Academy, the girls' Catholic school in Little Rock. Joshua was unconscious and appeared to be sleeping during their visit. I thanked them for their courage to come and visit their friend, given Joshua's current state. While Seth and Jaci came to Joshua's bedside to talk to him and hold his hand, Hannah held back. I think she was struggling with the emotion of it all; someone she had known since she was five years old was lying motionless and unresponsive in a hospital bed. Since I was in a wheelchair I couldn't easily put my arm around her, but I told her I understood and that it was okay. Jaci's voice, which is very distinctive, was one of the few things Joshua remembered from his time at UAMS.

Father James West, who had been our priest at Immaculate Conception Catholic Church, was now serving a parish in Texarkana, Arkansas, two hours away, yet he visited Joshua two or three times a week. We had first met him in 2001, after his first Mass at our church. He shook Joshua's hand and asked him his name and age. Joshua replied, "Joshua. Five." That was the beginning of a wonderful relationship for us.

As Joshua matured, he served as an altar boy at Mass and was one of a few boys Father West selected to help with funerals and other special events. He even served at the ordination of a new Bishop upon Father West's recommendation. Joshua had stayed connected to him through the years. They had a special relationship based on deep love and respect. Also, they had both been born in Texas. Having faith and Texas in common makes for a pretty strong bond. Father West's Arkansas license plate read TEXAS1.

When Father West wasn't visiting, he always held Joshua in his prayers. At one point a priest who traveled to parishes throughout the country with a display of religious artifacts came to Father West's parish in Texarkana. Father West asked if they could both pray for Joshua in the presence of the religious artifacts, all of which had a miraculous history documented by the Catholic Church.

During his first visit to UAMS, Father West pulled me aside to ask how I was doing and to assure me the accident was not my fault and that I shouldn't carry that burden with me. I'm not sure I had come to grips with that at the time, but his words were reassuring. One thing was for sure: if I let that burden be my focus, I would eventually rot from the inside out.

While Gwen left Joshua's side briefly on only two occasions, I was volun-told to go somewhere so I could lie down and not have to sleep in a chair. My nephew Greg Moody and his wife, Sha, my other nephew Micah Lock and his wife, Jess, and my niece Kelly Cannon and her husband, Joe, took turns caring for me.

Some evenings, one of them picked me up at the hospital and took me back the next morning. They fed me, provided a bed or sofa to sleep on, and provided some social interaction, which always involved laughter. It temporarily took my mind off the hospital. Although Gwen always insisted I leave overnight and sleep in a comfortable bed, a part of me felt guilty about leaving her at the hospital.

It wasn't easy to get into vehicles from a wheelchair. I was given a transition board that allowed me to slide out of the chair and onto another surface. It worked great as long as the surface I was moving to was close to the height of the wheelchair seat. I had to step up (definitely against doctor's orders) into SUVs and sometimes just slid into the back floorboard, then push myself up to a seat. Like our house, their houses were not designed for wheelchair mobility. When necessary, I'd crawl on the floor to the bathroom and lift myself up onto the toilet. I gained tremendous respect for folks who face these challenges daily.

A few days after Joshua was moved to the trauma floor, he was sitting up in his bed when he coughed—hard—and brought up blood. It startled and scared us. We immediately called the nurses, and they swung into action. In a matter of seconds, Joshua was wheeled down the hall to surgery.

As it turned out, Dr. Ron Robertson was the doctor treating Joshua that afternoon. He was a professor, a surgeon, and the head of the UAMS Trauma Program. After about forty-five minutes, Dr. Robinson came out to tell us everything was okay. He said Joshua's hard cough had most likely caused some scar tissue in his throat to bleed. As it turned out, this was a minor incident, but after our experiences in the previous weeks we were constantly on edge.

———— • ————

We were connected to Father Joseph Chan by Joshua's neurosurgeon, Dr. Rodriguez. We first met Father Joseph when he arrived at our hospital room to visit Joshua. Dressed in priest attire, he was a mature man of Asian descent, small in stature, and soft spoken. His calm demeanor gave us an immediate sense of peace. He greeted Gwen and me briefly and moved immediately to Joshua's bedside. We gave him his space. He paused briefly to survey the array of medical equipment, bags of medication, and sensors connected to Joshua. He placed his hands on Joshua's head and began to pray over him. After what seemed like several minutes, he leaned into Joshua, looked in his eyes, which were open at that point, and whispered something. After a final blessing, he turned to us and said, "Joshua is going to be okay."

After visiting and praying with us for a few more minutes Father Joseph departed. We never bothered to ask him what he had whispered to Joshua. He told us later that he had given Joshua the last rites, as is customary in these situations, but when he was able to look in Joshua's eyes, he felt he would recover. He whispered to Joshua that he would survive this with God's help.

We didn't know it at the time, but Father Joseph had spent twenty years as a medical doctor specializing in internal medicine, hospice, and palliative care. He was a doctor at Mercy Hospital in Fort Smith, Arkansas, when he decided to pursue the priesthood.

———— • ————

On March 10, 2013, around six o'clock in the morning, seminarian Joseph Chan packed his car in Fort Smith, Arkansas, to head back to Saint Meinrad Seminary in Indiana. The weather forecast predicted showers and thunderstorms.

(Sydney was a young nurse who cared for Joshua many times at UAMS. She is a great example of the talented, caring nurses we encountered. We consider her our friend, and she was kind enough to share her thoughts below.)

I'm not actually sure if y'all knew it at the time but Joshua was my first patient that I had off of orientation when I was a new grad nurse. I helped take care of him with my preceptor (Brooke) while on orientation then continued care when I came off of orientation. And I was always happy to see y'all under my name on the assignment board. I actually remember that there were a few nurses that had been outwardly less than optimistic and y'all had requested that they not care for Joshua and had provided a few names that you would prefer to take care of them given that they were scheduled. I made the list! And I remember being honored that I made the cut and that y'all trusted me with his care.

Complete transparency, when Joshua was with us on H4 at least for the first few weeks I wanted to stay positive and always hoped for a recovery for him but I didn't think things were going to go well. I thought if he recovered at all it wouldn't resemble the life that he was used to or that y'all were used to. He had almost no reactions or purposeful movement the majority of the time that I took care of him. I remember you and Gwen asking me how I thought he was doing and all I could say was "he's just taking baby steps but sometimes baby steps are big steps especially in the ICU." Which I meant and I still stand by to this day.

He was so intensely damaged neurologically but the two of you literally never lost faith. It may have wavered but you only let that show in your weakest or most exhausted moments. I remember thinking that it was amazing how strong your faith was but that I was afraid it was setting you up for a serious fall because of how serious his brain swelling was. But I wanted him to recover so badly and showed up every day happy to be assigned to you and to do anything I could to help him move the right direction. I honestly don't feel like I did just a heck of a lot but it was unreal to be involved in an actual miracle.

I don't want it to sound like I was just walking through the motions of caring for him or didn't think there was any hope at all. I knew there was a chance he'd be able to surprise us and I did my best to care for him for each 12-hour shift that I had with him but from a medical standpoint I knew too much to be entirely optimistic. He's so lucky to have you and Gwen as his faithfully optimistic support team.

His car hydroplaned out of control near Rolla, Missouri. The police report noted that the car hit a signpost along Interstate 44, veered toward the steel guardrail, took out at least eight posts of the guardrail, and flipped before coming to rest in a muddy field.

Joseph was rushed to Phelps County Hospital. The paramedics and emergency staff in the hospital resuscitated him with intravenous fluids and transfused him with many units of blood. He had multiple orthopedic fractures of the ribs, vertebrae, pelvis, sacrum, right leg, and radius in his left forearm. The rib fractures had punctured his lungs. His spleen was damaged, his liver was lacerated, and he had internal bleeding in his chest and abdomen. The CT scans revealed a traumatic brain injury and a hemorrhage in the right side of his brain. The decision was made to transport him to Mercy Hospital in Saint Louis, a specialty trauma center, by ambulance due to the poor weather conditions. At this point, Joseph was in a coma.

With so many injuries, his recovery took many months. He graduated from the seminary in May 2016 and became a priest. His second assignment was the Cathedral of Saint Andrew, the oldest place of worship in the city of Little Rock and the home church of our Bishop. He had only been a priest for a year and a half before our accident and had been at the Cathedral a little over a year.

In the months that followed, Father Joseph met with us, prayed with us, and offered numerous Mass intentions and special prayers for Joshua and our family. I now know that this wonderful priest who had come into our lives was there due to divine intervention.

So, let's recap. The doctor who performed Joshua's double craniectomy just happened to be on call that morning after returning to the rotation from a recent trip. She happened to be a woman of faith, a practicing Catholic, noticed the religious articles in Joshua's hospital room, and asked

Gwen if she'd like to pray over Joshua. Coincidentally, she attended a local cathedral and contacted a particular priest to come and visit Joshua, Gwen, and me. As it happened, the priest she contacted, Father Joseph, had not only served as a medical doctor but had survived a traumatic brain injury, crushed pelvis, and a host of other injuries from a near-fatal car crash just four years earlier. It was pretty easy to see God's hand in those relationships and series of events.

———◆———

Dr. Paul Wendel and his wonderful wife, Kathy, were so supportive during this period. We'd known the Wendels for years. We first met when their son, Daniel, and Joshua ended up on a soccer team when they were around eleven years of age—and eventually, attended Catholic High School together. The Wendels were a strong Catholic family. Paul, then a professor and doctor of obstetrics and gynecology in the Division of Maternal–Fetal Medicine at UAMS, had also delivered our second grandson. He was one of the first people to visit Joshua in the ICU and became a frequent visitor.

Paul is an anomaly as a senior doctor in a teaching hospital who is unafraid to share his deep Catholic faith when the opportunity presents itself. We were greeted by his positive attitude many mornings in the hospital. Paul would drop into Joshua's room a few times a week, give us a hug, talk to Joshua, pray with us, and ask if we needed anything. We just needed him to keep coming back. Paul's faith-filled, calm, positive demeanor was comforting to us. What a blessing he was! Kathy was behind the scenes, praying, posting supportive comments on CaringBridge, and making sure their five kids were doing what they were supposed to be doing. Before the kids came along, Kathy had a career as a critical care certified ICU nurse, a flight nurse on a helicopter, and an organ transplant coordinator.

Daniel Wendel was in a Benedictine seminary near Kansas City, Missouri, when he got the call from his father, Paul. Daniel says, "Dad was clearly emotional and had trouble getting the words out when he told me that Mr.

Moody and Josh were in a car accident." Daniel recalls being nervous about what his dad would say next, wondering if we had survived. "They were both injured, but both are alive. It doesn't look good for Josh," his dad said.

When Daniel got the call, he was about to enter a gathering of all eighty students at the seminary. As they entered the gathering space, one of the priests noticed that Daniel had a different demeanor than usual and inquired about it. "I explained the call I had just received, and this priest said, 'We'll all pray for them.'" Daniel says that "all eighty seminarians and priests prayed for the family on the spot. That was very powerful for me. Many of the seminarians came to me after that prayer and said they were going to devote holy hours for the family. Mass intentions and holy hours continued for months as Josh's recovery continued. Guys asked me routinely for an update on the recovery."

In early December, Daniel was home with his parents during a semester break and was able to visit Joshua in the hospital. At the time, Joshua was seldom fully conscious, as was the case during Daniel's visit. Daniel and his dad entered the room. I was in a wheelchair, and Joshua was lying still in his bed, eyes closed, connected to dozens of sensors, wires, and tubes. At that point he had a trach tube in his throat and braces on his feet and hands to keep him from posturing. Daniel recalls how hard it was to see his friend—a guy his age, a guy he spent hours with for years, either on the soccer field or in school—in that condition. "I remember thinking, how can a body go through this and still be alive?" he recalls.

"The fact that the seminarian community embraced this guy they didn't even know, that they continued to pray for him throughout his recovery, made me realize the power of communal prayer. That we really are all in it together," says Daniel.

Shortly after the accident, Tery Baskin was one of the first people I called. Tery was the founder and CEO of RxResults, a technology company in the pharmacy benefits industry. He was a faith-filled servant leader and successful businessman. Tery and Alan Gardner, the COO, had started the company years earlier. Alan was married to Stephanie, a vice-chancellor at UAMS at the time. Although I had gotten to know Alan through my consulting work with RxResults, we were not close friends, and Gwen had only met Stephanie once at a Christmas party.

After I contacted Tery, he got word to Stephanie, and she reached out to us. Prior to the accident, most everyone at RxResults knew about Joshua. He was in the local news periodically due to his entrepreneurial pursuits, and I spoke about him at the office on occasion. Stephanie contacted me to offer her help and guidance if we needed anything at UAMS. It's not that often that patients have a vice-chancellor of a major hospital come visit them in their room.

I don't remember the specifics of the first phone conversation I had with Stephanie after the accident. There were so many calls, visits, and texts that I can't tell you how many communications we've had. During our stay at UAMS—and beyond—she has been a consistent source of guidance, connection, and prayer. She connected us with doctors at UAMS and other facilities, and she aided in our decision making. She did all this with humility, a sense of service, and always with prayer.

Tery Baskin passed away less than two years after our accident following a long bout with cancer. I still miss him. Tery had set all these relationships in motion many years earlier when he hired me to consult with his company. At the time, it was a blessing just to be engaged with RxResults during a significant time in their development. That blessing has continued through the relationships forged during my service there. I will always believe God had a hand in how that has all worked out and that He blessed us by putting such wonderful people like Tery, Alan, and Stephanie in our lives.

A few weeks into Joshua's stay at UAMS, Emily Anne Gray popped into his room and introduced herself as his speech therapist. She asked a few background questions and started trying to engage Joshua. Although his eyes were open, he was not fully conscious. This did not stop Emily Anne. She talked to him as if he was fully alert and pushed him to respond. She got a thumbs-up, but that was about it. Despite this minimal response, she was positive about helping him recover. We began to look forward to Emily Anne's therapy sessions. Her caring, upbeat attitude was contagious.

We asked our new friend Katie Keine (one of the social workers we encountered and friend of our dear Father West) if she could connect us to other caregivers who had loved ones with similar conditions and had decided to have them rehab at any of the out-of-state facilities we were beginning to hear about. We spoke to several families with tragic stories about their kids or young adult children. All of their injured children had survived. Some were still recovering years later. Others had recovered well enough to attend college and have careers and families despite their remaining challenges. One of those people was Jacki Bruning. Jacki and her husband David's son, Jon David, had been paralyzed in a diving accident.

Someone had already asked Jacki if she would speak to me before I called. Jacki was as caring and open as she could be. She answered every question and offered heartfelt support for us. While at UAMS, we communicated with Jacki many times via calls and text. She shared her strong faith with us as well, and that was most comforting.

Joshua was improving—less storming and a few more thumbs-up responses. He had survived so far, but we were not sure if he'd advance.

A little over three weeks into our stay at UAMS, Katie Keine informed us that it would soon be time to discharge Joshua and that his only option for rehab was a nursing home.

Jacki Bruning was especially wonderful to us. She shared her time with us on the phone, commented frequently on our CaringBridge posts, and visited us in the hospital. She gave us a copy of *Jesus Calling*, a daily devotional written by Sarah Young that we continue to read on a daily basis. Someone had given her this book when one of her boys was injured, and it made such an impact on her that she passes it along whenever she can. It is written as though Jesus is speaking directly to you with guidance and scripture for the day. While it may be that anyone in our situation would find those readings aligned with their immediate needs, I choose to believe that it was just one more example of how God was giving us what we needed when we needed it.

You may have read about the Tullier family and their son, Nick, who was one of the law enforcement officers shot in an ambush in Louisiana in 2016. Nick was treated at TIRR, and I visited with his dad, James, frequently. Nick's injuries were severe. He survived until his passing in 2022.

Finally, the Durham family. The story of James Durham is on the wall at TIRR, and his journey from accident to recovery is amazing. James formed the nonprofit TBIOneLove and speaks to TBI patients and groups around the country. To give you a sense of how he has turned his deadly motorcycle accident into a positive, *TBI* in the name of the organization does not stand for traumatic brain injury. It stands for This Beautiful Injury. Yes, you read it correctly. I referred to his accident as "deadly." His heart stopped six times. James says as traumatic as it was, he wouldn't change a thing. James's mother, Liz Durham, was a great support to Gwen while she and Joshua were in Houston. Gwen's younger sister, Gloria Rouly, introduced us to her. Another miraculous connection.

—◆—

TIRR, affiliated with Memorial Hermann Health Center and ranked second in the country for TBI rehab, is located in the Texas Medical Center (TMC) in Houston alongside world-renowned medical facilities such as the M.D. Anderson Cancer Center. Other major institutions include Texas Children's Hospital, Baylor College of Medicine, Houston Methodist Hospital, St. Luke's Health, Memorial Hermann–Texas Medical Center, and the University of Texas Health Sciences Center. That impressed us, as did the cutting-edge research and technology available at TIRR. It is one of the few facilities in the country with a Disorders of Consciousness program that focuses on rehabbing patients who are not fully conscious as a result of traumatic brain injuries.

We had lived in the Houston area for five years when I worked as an aerospace consultant, a senior program analyst for the Johnson Space Center, and later started my own company. That had been quite a few years earlier, and we had not stayed in routine contact with the friends we made while living there. We weren't even sure if most of them were still in the area. In addition, since TIRR did not have residences for the family in their facility or nearby, Gwen would either have to stay in the room with Joshua and use the pullout sofa and bathroom, or rent an apartment near TIRR since she didn't know her way around the city. We had no idea how we would cover apartment rent and living expenses, especially near the Texas Medical Center, where rent was higher and you paid for parking everywhere you went.

We had decided that since we were now on my insurance and my salary was the highest, Gwen would accompany Joshua to rehab, wherever it might be. We had no idea what that meant exactly, and the time frame was open-ended. There were many more questions than answers at that point. How would we afford the out-of-pocket living expenses? How long would the rehab take? If the rehab facility didn't have residential accommodations, where would Gwen live, and how would she travel in a strange city? What would happen with her teaching job? The unknowns were endless and, if we had focused on them, would have made us feel hopeless. We could not let that happen. We had already figured out that this journey was a marathon, not a sprint, and that we had to be patient and keep moving forward despite not knowing what lay ahead.

We'd been living in Joshua's room at UAMS for nearly a month already. We had a sense of what to expect. A few weeks on that sofa bed is tolerable in a desperate situation, but how would Gwen handle it for many months if necessary? As if sleeping on a less-than-comfortable bed was not enough, the pace of the trauma ward in a hospital is not conducive to high-quality sleep. As we had already experienced at UAMS, lack of sleep, unfamiliar surroundings, and a high-stress situation can take a toll on you. Our challenge was that we had no connection to TIRR, and neither did UAMS.

We were seriously considering both facilities. Shepherd was very accommodating, even sending a representative to answer all our questions. It certainly seemed like a good option for Joshua. They were evaluating us as we were evaluating them. These programs had limited beds available, and they were selective about who they offered them to. As with most programs like this, they wanted patients who could pay and who would have the greatest likelihood of success. Their private donors, grant funders, insurance companies, certifying organizations, and patient families all scrutinize the data reflecting their success.

<hr />

As we were in the middle of the discernment process, Joshua was stable enough to move from the ICU to the trauma ward at UAMS. While we were happy for the progress, we knew we would have to start over with a new set of nurses and doctors. We had already figured out that we knew Joshua better than they did, despite all their medical data, and needed to advise them on his response to certain treatments.

The morning after Joshua moved to the trauma floor, we were up early to greet the doctor in charge that day and their entourage of residents and students. As divine providence would have it, Joshua's doctor that morning was Dr. John Taylor. He began by asking a few of the common questions about how he was doing and checking his response to stimuli. The last question he asked was, "Is there anything else we can do for you?" I decided to mention that we were trying to decide on rehab facilities and that we had connections to Shepherd but not TIRR.

"So, you're considering sending him to TIRR?" he asked.

"Yes sir, but we don't know who to talk to there," I said.

"Wait just a minute." At that point, Dr. Taylor took his cell phone from his right front pocket and sent a text.

I didn't really think much about this at the moment because we already knew that the doctors carried multiple pagers and phones and received messages every few minutes all day long. I assumed that his phone had been vibrating in his pocket and that he was simply responding to a text.

After about a minute, Dr. Taylor said, "I just sent a text to the head of the program at TIRR. I used to work at Memorial Hermann and with the folks at TIRR. It's a great facility. You'll be hearing from them."

Let me recap. We were a little more than a week away from Joshua's release from the hospital. If we didn't relocate him to a rehab facility, he was coming home with us or going to a nursing home. A doctor we had never met happened to be on the schedule that week in the trauma unit. He had worked at TIRR and knew the director.

That text led to a phone call and a visit from their field representative, who flew in a few days later. We were, of course, impressed with what Tracy Bridges, the TIRR representative, had to say. As decision day approached, Shepherd's offer of a bed now had a deadline. That was understandable, since there is usually a waiting list for the top programs in the country, but it was unsettling because we were still conducting our due diligence. There was now a time limit on the most important decision we had ever had to make.

Once Shepherd set their deadline, we immediately contacted TIRR. To our surprise, our representative told us that their invitation to bring Joshua to TIRR had no time limit. While I was surprised and incredibly thankful, I was also curious why TIRR would offer that. Tracy's response was, "I don't know who talked to who, but Joshua is on a VIP list of some sort. I've been told that TIRR will take him whenever you all are ready." The text from Dr. Taylor had initiated a chain of events, among medical professionals with whom we had no connection, that had made it possible for Joshua to rehab at one of the finest facilities of its kind in the country.

At this point some of you may be thinking, *How lucky can you get?* or *What a wonderful coincidence!* Albert Einstein once said that "coincidence is God's way of remaining anonymous."

Even with the option of going to TIRR, we still had no solid connections in Houston to serve as a support system for Gwen—and no idea how we would pay for living expenses.

Enter the Davises. Or, as I like to call them, God's cavalry. We believe that divine intervention connected us. A sequence of events that had begun years earlier had led to what we fully expect to be a lifelong friendship.

Joshua had dated Audrey Davis for a while, and he had spent a fair amount of time with her parents, Joe and Robin, in Houston. They involved him in a number of family activities, treated him like another son, and got to know him well. Although Joshua and Audrey's long-distance relationship didn't last, Joshua and Joe still shared an interest in cars and business and communicated with each other periodically.

Gwen had called the Davises right after the accident to let them know about Joshua. That was the first time that Gwen and Robin had spoken at all. There had been texts back and forth while Joshua and Audrey were dating but never a phone conversation. Text and phone conversations continued between Gwen and the Davises in the first few days and weeks after the accident.

The Davises asked if they could come and visit about three weeks after the accident and approximately one week before Joshua was scheduled to be discharged from the hospital. We had still not made a decision about where he would go for rehab. Gwen and I welcomed the opportunity to finally meet Audrey's parents. They didn't know us but clearly loved Joshua and wanted to see him.

Joe had built a successful engineering firm in Houston, loved cars and technology, and had earned his pilot's license along the way. He piloted their trip up to Little Rock in a small plane. Upon their arrival in the hospital, we all hugged one another as though we had been friends for years. From that very first meeting, Gwen and I knew we were among kindred spirits with a strong faith and a deep love for Joshua.

Gwen had communicated to Robin that we were considering Houston as a possible rehab location. What we didn't know was that Robin's heart had opened to the idea of helping us. She felt that God had placed this opportunity before them and that she and her husband needed to act on it. As if you need any additional insight into the character of the Davises, they were focused on helping us while they, themselves, had been displaced by Hurricane Harvey. Harvey had hit the Houston area with a vengeance months earlier, and the Davises were temporarily living in an apartment while their home was being rebuilt. They already had plenty on their plate but somehow made room for the Moodys.

The Davises saw Joshua, and we all continued to visit in his room. After a while, Joe said, "We know that you all are considering coming to Houston for rehab. We just want you to know that God has put it on our hearts to help you all and Joshua. If you choose to come to Houston, we got you. Gwen, we will help you with accommodations, transportation, and whatever you need."

It is difficult to express how Gwen and I felt at that moment. We had been in anguish, praying about this most important decision regarding Joshua's rehab. The Davises' offer was like wrapping us in a warm blanket.

Feelings of relief, love, and thankfulness washed over us. Joshua was returning to his birthplace.

Once again, God Almighty had placed people in our path to help us.

Texas Bound

Wheels Up Tomorrow!

December 11, 2017: Well they told us when they contacted med flight that things would move quickly. They were right. Joshua and Gwen are scheduled to load up and depart for Houston TIRR at 11:30a tomorrow morning. This news is both scary and wonderful. We believe with all our heart that Joshua will flourish in the high tech, aggressive rehab environment of TIRR.

Gwen is nervous about all the last minute trip prep and making her way around in her new environment, but that will likely all subside tomorrow morning as she shifts into momma bear mode to manage the tasks ahead. We know that she will be an integral part of his rehab and she is the best person on earth to do it.

I will remain here to work and start my rehab in a week or so. I hope to travel to Houston as often as possible to support the effort. Although I know TIRR is the best place for Joshua, my heart aches just thinking of being away from Joshua and Gwen for what may be many months. However, I am very fortunate to have the love and support of our daughter Emily, our grandsons, and many friends and family. Very humbled and incredibly blessed.

We will continue to post as often as we can and maybe Gwen can provide some pictures as Joshua progresses. Please keep up the prayers. We depend on them.

A sample of the many responses we received from this post:

I am so excited things are moving forward with Josh's recovery. My prayers are with Gwen and Josh as they travel to Houston, where I know more prayers will be answered. David if you need anything, and I mean anything please don't hesitate to call the Simon's. We adore your family and are here for anything you need. God Bless you all!

—Amy Simon

The medical flight crew arrived in our room early on the morning of December 12. It was the birthday of Gwen's sweet mom, Genevieve. Gwen would miss the celebration. The lead nurse was friendly, matter of fact, and had an Australian accent. Other medical personnel helped with the logistics of loading Joshua onto the gurney for transport. This operation took some time since many of the tubes, wires, and sensors attached to him in the hospital had to be unattached from hospital equipment and reattached to transport equipment. In addition, he was strapped to the gurney, and they had placed one of those very attractive Styrofoam helmets on his head.

There were quite a few folks in the room that morning with family members, old friends, new friends, nurses, and the flight crew. It was a bit chaotic. We were most appreciative for the medical staff's leniency with us regarding visitors. Gwen was traveling on the plane with Joshua to Houston, so she had to be all packed and ready to go as well.

When Joshua left, it was time for me to leave the hospital permanently and return home. Even though I had been discharged weeks earlier, I had camped out at UAMS with Gwen and Joshua for the duration. Our friend Linda Bridges, one of Gwen's teaching mates, piled my wheelchair in her car and gave me a ride home—well, to our house. The folks who made it a home were on a plane to Houston.

The doctors, nurses, and medical staff at UAMS had become like an extended family for us in the last month. We had taken up residence in their place of work, and they could not have been more welcoming. Since we knew we would be leaving soon, we started saying our goodbyes days earlier. Since the shifts for doctors and nurses were always subject to change, we made sure to tell them goodbye, thank them, and give them a hug when we saw them over those last several days. While I knew we'd be back— after all, I'd made them a promise—I didn't know exactly when. Because medical professionals change shifts and jobs fairly frequently, we also knew we might never see some of these caregivers again. A few who stood out to us based on their medical knowledge and patient care included Dr. Mary Kimbrough, nurses Tiffani and Sydney, and of course, Nurse Ashley.

While I was excited and hopeful for Joshua to take this next step in his recovery, I was anxious about the flight. A lot can go wrong when you take a TBI patient up to 30,000 feet for a few hours. We signed every waiver known to man. What if the change in pressure affected his brain? What if he needed emergency surgery or some sort of extensive procedure? What if bad weather or turbulence during the flight put him at risk? What if …? What if …? What if I just let God handle it?

An ambulance took Joshua from UAMS to the airplane waiting on the tarmac at Clinton National Airport. Gwen wasn't allowed to ride in the back with Joshua during the fifteen-minute trip. Father West met Gwen and Joshua at the plane. He didn't ask anyone's permission to be there. He was on a mission. He said a blessing over Joshua before they put him on the plane and also blessed the crew and the pilots. He told the pilots they had some very precious cargo and to please get him and Gwen to Houston safely.

Gwen recalls, "The plane was crowded. I was strapped into a jump seat and sat at Joshua's feet. Two medical techs monitored him. One sat near his head, and the other sat behind me where most of the monitoring equipment was located. Joshua lay on the gurney. He was sedated, but his eyes were open. He seemed to be aware of where he was. We got a thumbs-up from him. I held his hand for most of the flight."

The flight took several hours. The plane landed at Hobby Airport in Houston. Joshua was taken off the plane and transferred to an ambulance for the last few miles of the trip to TIRR. Again, Gwen rode in the front seat of the ambulance. It was very difficult for her to not be next to him during these ambulance rides.

When Gwen arrived at TIRR with Joshua that afternoon she was greeted by Robin Davis. The Davises had said they would "be there" for us in Houston, but Gwen had no idea that Robin would literally be there when she arrived. It was a blessing to find a friendly face waiting there for her.

Robin brought a care basket with all sorts of things for Gwen and stayed with them until early evening. The TIRR staff was friendly and welcoming. They wasted no time in checking Joshua in, getting him to a room, completing his profile, and discussing the therapy schedule for the next day. Gwen and Deanna Bennett, the day shift charge nurse, hit it off immediately. Deanna was very friendly, knowledgeable and empathetic.

We were feeling good about our decision to come to TIRR. It all felt right. Until it didn't.

The Top of the Roller Coaster

Gwen and I have always liked roller coasters. We rode on small ones as kids and much bigger and faster ones at Disney and other theme parks after we had children. On every roller coaster I've ridden there is a time about halfway through the ride when the cars climb slowly to the highest point on the ride. It's a brief sense of calm following the thrilling first half of the ride. As you approach the top of the ride the calm is replaced by anticipation and a bit of anxiety. It's a roller coaster, so you know there is a big drop, a sharp curve, a three-sixty loop—or all three—on the other side of the high point. The difference between a roller coaster and our real-world situation is that, while we were experiencing the brief calm and anticipation of what lay ahead, we had no idea what would come next. As it turned out, it was wilder than any thrill ride we could imagine. Hold on to the bar, boys and girls. Here we go!

Late at night, just hours after his arrival at TIRR, Joshua's vitals began to show signs of trouble. Gwen noticed the fluctuations first—she'd seen this phenomenon many times by now—and called for a nurse to come to the room. The nurse dismissed it at first, but Gwen was persistent. She'd been at Joshua's side now for weeks and knew as much about signs of trouble as any medical professional. After Gwen called the nurse into his room multiple times and questioned her, she realized that Gwen was right and called in other nurses and staff to intervene with Joshua.

I received a call from Gwen late in the evening. She was crying and frantic but trying to remain calm so she could tell me what was happening. It was my first full day at home since the accident a month earlier. I was confined to a wheelchair and had spent the afternoon rearranging our furniture so I could get around and trying to determine how I was going to go to the bathroom when my chair was six inches wider than the door. I was also looking through a stack of mail taller than the triple stack at IHOP, mostly medical bills, and trying to figure out how I could get started back to work. I was already in the negative on annual sick leave.

Joshua's condition continued to worsen, and by two o'clock that morning he was in full blown storming mode. His heart raced at over 140 beats per minute, he had trouble breathing, and his temperature was over 102 degrees despite rotating doses of Tylenol and ibuprofen. These episodes could last hours, and this one was the worst yet. Gwen recalls, "There were a half dozen doctors, nurses, and other staff at Joshua's bedside and in and out of the room for most of the night. I just sat on the sofa bed, a few feet away, wringing my hands and crying. At one point I squeezed in beside one of the doctors near the head of the bed. I leaned down and spoke quietly into Joshua's ear that everything was going to be okay, that I was here with him, so was God, and that the doctors and nurses were here to help him. I had no idea if he could hear or understand what I was telling him. I just knew that both of us needed to know that."

Joshua's condition began to improve and by six that morning he was somewhat stabilized. They took Joshua to get a CT scan. Lisa, the head nurse from the third floor, came up to help. She was very warm and caring. She hugged Gwen, got her some coffee, and told her to call if she needed anything. Later, Gwen was informed by the doctor that the scan showed something on the right side of Joshua's brain. The medical staff was concerned enough after reviewing results from various tests and scans to recommend that Joshua be transported to Memorial Hermann's Emergency Care facility, around the corner from TIRR, for immediate observation. Gwen met Dr. Sunil Kothari, Joshua's doctor and the medical director of TIRR's Disorders of Consciousness program, briefly that morning. They didn't have much time to visit before Joshua was transported to Memorial Hermann's ER by ambulance, but he connected Gwen with Dr. Ryan Kitagawa, a neurosurgeon at Memorial Hermann.

This trip of just a few blocks was not quick or easy. Joshua had to be transferred onto a gurney and transported by ambulance, with all of his monitoring equipment still connected, several blocks to one of the largest and busiest hospitals in the world, taken off the ambulance, checked in, and assessed. Gwen had all her luggage for an extended stay in Joshua's room at TIRR. In addition to dealing with Joshua's medical emergency, she also had to consider the logistics of her situation. How long would she be at Memorial Hermann? Could she stay in his room? Did she need to take all of her belongings with her, or could she leave them at TIRR? Once again, Gwen had all of the hard decisions and unknowns on her shoulders, and I wasn't there to help and support.

While this was concerning, unexpected, and unsettling, Gwen arrived at Memorial Hermann with enough belongings, and mentally prepared, for a few days of observation. Upon arrival, she was informed that the ER medical staff had seen the results of the tests and scans and that they were preparing to take Joshua to surgery immediately. Scans revealed that blood was pooling in the top-back-right region between his skull and brain, creating significant pressure and potentially causing additional injury to his brain. The procedure to drill a hole in his skull to drain the pooling blood was not a suggestion. It was required and needed to be done immediately.

Gwen felt as though everything was going on around her and she was not in control of any of it. Not long after checking into the ER they were moved out of the waiting room and into another area. A nurse came to her and said they were prepping Joshua for surgery. She didn't provide any other details. Someone else came to her and asked her to sign paperwork. One of the forms was a Do Not Resuscitate (DNR). At that point, she lost it. Gwen had likely signed a DNR for his previous surgery at UAMS but had no recollection of doing so. To suddenly be confronted with the stark reality and weight of this decision was overwhelming. She called me.

This was a tough call for both of us. Joshua's potential quality of life and what he might want were weighing heavily on her. All those feelings of this not being the son she had birthed, raised, and loved came flooding back. All those questions about what his life might be like if he didn't recover, and whether he wanted that kind of life, were swirling around in her head. Would it be better if he didn't have to face all that? Would it be better if we didn't have to watch him face it? We might be caring for him for the rest of his life. What if he outlived us? Gut-wrenching questions that no human, and especially no parent, wants to have to decide. If you are forced to decide, you'd want weeks to work through it with family, friends, doctors, and pastors. We didn't have weeks. We had minutes.

I did not have the burden of confusion that held Gwen in its grip. I had decided a few days after his initial surgery at UAMS that God had his healing hands on Joshua and that he would recover. I didn't have much evidence to back that up except that Joshua had already had a few opportunities to leave this world and he was still here. I also didn't know what the definition of "recovery" actually meant. I just believed it with all my heart and soul. My earlier vision of Joshua and Jesus doing some rewiring was what helped me be positive every day.

After Gwen and I talked for a few minutes, she began to regain her composure. She knew what I believed, and she believed it as well. She'd been blindsided by this decision, and it had put her in a temporary tailspin. She just needed me to help her decide. I was adamant that she not sign the DNR. She didn't.

They took Joshua back to surgery, and Gwen went to the waiting room. "I was feeling scared and alone," she remembers, "so I called Robin. I also sent texts to family members and called Deanna at TIRR. Fortunately, she was still there after her shift was over. Although we'd just met, she listened to me, consoled me, and offered to send someone over to me, or come herself when she could. Robin arrived not long after my call and stayed with me. We didn't talk much. Just having Robin there, someone who knew and loved Joshua, did as much to comfort me as was possible at that time. What a blessing!"

My post on CaringBridge included this plea:

> Wherever you are and whatever you are doing right
> now, please stop and take a minute to pray for Joshua and
> for Gwen.

We didn't know it at the time, but Robin had been keeping a journal since she and Joe met with us in Little Rock. Robin recalls that Gwen called the morning of December 13 and said they were taking Joshua to emergency surgery to drain fluid from his brain. Robin traveled to the hospital, arriving around ten. She found Gwen crying in the waiting room. She was crying because she had not signed the DNR form for Joshua and likely also from pure exhaustion. They talked about what all had happened and prayed.

When Dr. Kitagawa came out of surgery, he said the drainage procedure went smoothly.

This crisis was behind us, but I couldn't help feeling as though the days ahead would likely include challenging decisions and uncharted waters for us. We knew we were in God's hands. We prayed for patience and strength, and we knew we would get what we needed when we needed it.

I called Joshua on FaceTime not long after he regained consciousness from his surgery. He was clearly still a bit groggy, but he reportedly gave one of the nurses a thumbs-up. During our call, I got the most obvious smile I had seen. We prayed for a restful night and next few days in ICU as the medical team observed Joshua for further complications. While it had been a nerve-wracking day of difficult conversations, we knew that God Almighty had His healing hand on us and was watching over the medical team as well.

I asked our friends and family to please keep the love and prayers coming because our ability to withstand the stress of this situation depended on it. We received periodic responses to my CaringBridge posts that lifted us up, as did this one:

> David, your posts are God's work in action.
> —Kristine Barnello

Joshua experienced some neurostorming following the surgery, but much less than the previous night. This meant that Gwen also rested better in the plush, super-king bed of the ICU. (Just kidding. It was none of those things.) Joshua remained in Memorial Hermann, around the corner from TIRR, as they continued to assess his condition.

The morning after surgery, a physical therapist and an occupational therapist had Joshua sitting up on the side of his bed despite his apparent grogginess. He didn't respond much to them at first. He didn't seem to have the strength to raise his head. The therapists felt that Joshua could do what they asked him to do and expected him to do it. One of the therapists used her hands to push his head up. He reached up to try and push her hands away. When they laid him back down, Gwen told me that he raised his head to try to sit back up. I prayed daily that these were signs that his fighting spirit was still intact. We knew he would need every bit of his natural drive and work ethic to get through this journey.

> Woohoo for sitting up on the edge of bed! I look forward to reading more posts with good news. Keep up the hard work, Josh!!
>
> —*Emily Anne*

From Day One in Houston, in true God fashion, Gwen had had the support of our new friends Robin and Joe. They were a tremendous help to us in this transition. I think we are friends for life now. God has put some tremendous people in our path already. I pray that we can be those people in the path of others as this journey plays out.

In an entry in her own journal, Robin commented that she and Gwen met Josh's nurse, Anthony. Anthony was going to school to be a nurse practitioner. Robin said that she didn't believe it was a coincidence that he was Josh's nurse. She believed Anthony was placed there by God. He was very attentive and caring and very knowledgeable, more than a typical nurse.

According to Robin, at around three-thirty on the afternoon of December 14, after Joshua had been bathed, Gwen noticed that his oxygen level was dropping. He looked stressed. The surgery to relieve the pressure on his brain had been performed the day before, and his ability to communicate had already improved. Gwen asked him if he was hurting. He gave a thumbs-up, and she asked, "Where?" He moved his left hand toward his chest. She asked again to verify, and again, he moved his hand toward his chest. When his oxygen began to reach more dangerous levels the ICU team went into emergency mode.

In a scene that had now become all too familiar, doctors and nurses surrounded Joshua's bed. Robin was with Gwen, and they were asked to leave his room. They stepped out into the hallway. The curtain in Joshua's hallway window was drawn, but Robin found a slight opening so she could see what was going on inside the room. Gwen didn't want to see and turned her back away from the window. It was all hands on deck, including Dr. Kitagawa.

The doctor came into the hallway and told Gwen that Joshua could have blood clots in his lungs and that he would need to be on a breathing machine. That concerned both Gwen and Robin, and they began to cry. Robin watched what was going on in the room through the opening in the curtain while Gwen was on the phone with me, communicating what was going on. "It was so hard to see Josh having such a hard time," Robin recalls. "His body was limp, and everyone was around the bed. Someone was even standing on the bed pushing the tube down his throat into his lungs." Joshua fought back against the pain of the procedure. After several minutes, they identified several blood clots in his lungs and worked feverishly to remove them, which they did.

Robin recalls thinking that only time would tell if further damage had been done. We couldn't worry about that at the time. We could only say a prayer of thanks for the doctors and nurses—and pray that Joshua returned to a stable medical condition over the next few days.

After this latest health scare, I recall thinking that Joshua was still here for a reason. We could only hope we would live long enough for God to reveal what that reason was. Some of the reasons were already obvious, with the rekindling of relationships with dear friends, closer ties with family members, and connections to new friends whose paths we likely never would have crossed.

This was a journey of faith, patience, strength, and hope, and we had only just begun. It was already clear that this journey, no matter where it led, would be an emotional roller coaster that would test all of us in some way or another. Gwen and I had no choice but to make the full journey, but we realized that some folks would need to step off from time to time—maybe even permanently—to take a break. That was completely understandable and exactly why so many people were involved. It would take all of us to see this through to the end. While we appreciated the love and support we got directly from so many, we also needed to love and support one another as friends and caregivers bound together by a common mission. Those loving, faith-filled relationships may be the longest lasting legacy of the journey with Joshua, spanning decades and generations. What a tremendous blessing that will be.

My CaringBridge post solicited a number of heartfelt and uplifting responses:

> We will never stop praying for Josh and your family. He is a special young man and God is working through him in so many ways. Love you all. Wish I could give Gwen a big hug!
>
> —*Amy Simon*

> Praying for Josh, your entire family and his medical team. He has touched so many in such a short time. May God be with all of you.
>
> —*Laura McCammon*

> You are so right David!!! Josh is here for a reason and one day he will tell his journey. We continue to lift you all up in our prayers! Thank you and Gwen for keeping us posted. Please tell Gwen to take care of herself too. The caregiver needs TLC too ?
>
> —*Diane Ford*

Thank you for the updates David. I imagine you don't always feel up to writing and/or sharing such difficult details. I can tell you that my family is following Josh's story closely and it's already had a profound impact on us. We pray for him, hurt with you, and have hope that he will make a full recovery. Fight like hell Josh. We are all pulling for you!

—*Aaron & Emily*

Stay the course—it's already plotted—God's got this—

—*patti drake*

After the blood clot scare, Dr. Kitagawa spoke with us (I joined by phone) about putting Joshua's skull flaps back in. It had been just over a month since Dr. Rodriguez had removed them at UAMS, five days after the accident, to avoid further brain damage due to swelling. The flaps were in sanitary storage at UAMS in Little Rock. We were told when they were removed that it would likely be several months before they were put back in place. They wanted to be absolutely sure that all swelling had subsided before they put them back in.

Dr. Kitagawa told us that the skin on Joshua's forehead was pressing against his brain where the skull flaps were missing. "Flaps" seems like such an informal and overly simplified term for pieces of the skull. But Dr. Kitagawa explained that the brain and skull actually work as a system to protect the brain and that, for the system to work properly, it needed to be fully intact. This made total sense to me, having worked in engineering environments. When a system that was designed to be integrated is operating in an unintegrated state, although there may be work-arounds, it doesn't perform as expected, and things just go wrong. Joshua's cranial system had to be returned, as close as possible, to its original integrated divine design.

Joshua's original skull flaps were in sanitary storage back in Little Rock. Using them was not an option, given the risky logistics of transporting Joshua to UAMS. Also, neurosurgeons prefer not to use flaps they haven't removed and for which they have not controlled the chain of custody. Clearly, the surgery should be done at Memorial Hermann. Dr. Kitagawa also explained that the flaps could be made from either of three kinds of materials. The molded mesh material would be molded in real time by the surgeon during the surgery. This material was used quite often, had a slight risk of post-op infection, and could be used immediately. Titanium was, well, titanium.

Our other option was something called a PEEK implant. Fabricated from Polyetheretherketone (PEEK) by a German company, these customized implants are designed individually for each patient to replace bony voids in the cranial and craniofacial skeleton. The PEEK implant is measured precisely by lasers, custom fit, stronger than mesh, and has less risk of post-op infection—but could take weeks to arrive from the German manufacturer. Waiting at least two weeks for delivery was an issue. That would further delay the start of his rehab at TIRR, and he would remain at risk of further brain issues while we waited.

As a hardware designer, lover of German-engineered autos, and a custom-fit kind of guy, I thought—and Gwen agreed—this was exactly what Joshua would want.

Dr. Kitagawa said he had a close contact who owed him a favor and he would see what he could do. Joshua was measured for the PEEK implants. They arrived three days later. I think this is what is meant by the phrase "God's speed."

———◆◆———

Following the recent stress and challenges, Joshua and Gwen had a restful night. That morning Joshua was moving all of his extremities more than he had since the accident and seemed more alert than ever. I asked our friends and family to pray for a day of peace and healing for Joshua and Gwen. Robin had been with them since their arrival in Houston. Gwen's sister Gloria, also known as the "fun" sister, arrived from north Texas to support them until the following week. Gwen's other sister, Cindy, had been by our side often at UAMS and was always organizing behind the scenes. We were blessed in abundance with friends and family to help and support us. Our new friend Jacki Bruning, who has had similar medical challenges in her family, sent this in a text: *We are given this life because we are strong enough to live it.* Exactly what we needed to hear at the time.

My reading that morning became my prayer for all of us that day: "May the God of hope fill you with all joy and peace as you trust in him, so that you may overflow with hope by the power of the Holy Spirit."—Romans 15:13

Joshua continued to improve after the surgery to remove fluid from his brain. He was able to sit in a chair wearing a protective helmet. Both eyes began opening more. There was more movement, and he continued to communicate with Gwen regarding how he felt by using thumbs-up or thumbs-down responses—all of this without the rehab focus that he would eventually get at TIRR. Joshua was moved from ICU to a step-down room at that point and to a trauma floor room after that. All this moving from room to room was unsettling but, as Gwen reminded me, it was happening because of his continued improvement.

I was in awe of Joshua's ability to withstand these emergency procedures—and the pain associated with neurostorming episodes—and somehow bounce back and continue to improve. There was no question that God had His healing hand on him.

We anticipated the arrival of Joshua's custom-fit skull flaps soon and, if his medical condition was good, a surgery to install them. This procedure would restore the system surrounding the brain. We were hopeful that the restoration of Joshua's skull would also improve the flow of spinal fluid around his brain and stop it from pooling and putting pressure on his brain.

While I was still in a wheelchair at this point, I was hopeful my surgeon would release me early the coming week so I could begin therapy. Oh yeah, and then there was my work. My boss and work team at the Small Business Administration had been great! People I'd never met from other parts of the agency donated their annual leave to me so I could continue getting paid while recovering. Amazing! However, it was time to return to help my team. I couldn't have asked for more support, especially from my colleagues Suzanne Terrazas and Daniel Salman.

Daniel was our Administrative Officer in the SBA District Office. He was a Swiss army knife, handling veterans' programs, IT, and a host of other responsibilities. He made sure that all the paperwork and requests regarding my leave were properly filed. I'm sure this required hours of phone calls and bureaucratic paperwork. I wouldn't know. All I did was sign a few papers that he brought to the hospital. In addition to his prayers, this was a wonderful gift to us. It allowed me to focus on my family.

I was planning to travel to Houston for that surgery. In the meantime, my family—Kelly and Joe, Micah and Jess, and Greg and Sha—stepped up again and took great care of me. The love and support from our church, family, and friends was tremendous. This support was very important as I began my transition back to work and, very soon, my rehab.

We were so incredibly blessed with support. Responses to my posts:

> We had 22 youth leaders praying for Josh at the Diocese today. We prayed for complete restoration of his health and for peace and comfort for you and Gwen.
>
> —*Liz Tingquist*

> David, it's great you keep us posted. We spoke to Father John about Joshua today and we will continue praying. We know that God is in control. As Father told us God is with us through everything that happens to us and there

is always a reason. We must continue to trust Him. Give Gwen and Joshua our love.

—*Sonya Coco*

This is such positive news! Almost 53 years ago my father was involved in a head-on accident with a semi tractor on a bridge. His only injuries were severe head trauma and a lacerated ear. He spent four months in the hospital and several months rehabbing. Medicine has come so far since then I can't help but believe God has a remarkable plan for Joshua! Love to you all!

—*Monica, Travis, Alec and Zach Reiners*

In my CaringBridge posts I asked everyone to please pray for the doctors and nurses during the upcoming multiple-hour surgery. I also asked for prayers that Joshua would be strong and that he could handle whatever happened during surgery. We had already been amazed at his ability to handle emergency medical procedures and bounce back rather quickly. His will to live and make progress was inspiring. We were constantly reminded that all things are possible if we let God take the lead.

I reminded folks tracking us on CaringBridge that we appreciated and felt each prayer they sent our way. Their prayers and God's love were like warm blankets to us in those days of insecurity and stress. Even in emergency situations, we knew that we were not alone and we were wrapped in God's love. That peace and comfort was everything to us.

I got chills reading this! What miraculous things are happening each and every day. Thank you for these updates and you all continue to be in our prayers.

—*Nancy Thomas*

I teared up reading this! God is so good!! Keep up the hard work, Josh! I'm so proud of you!!

—*Emily Anne*

Beautiful words and so true...warm blanket indeed! So thrilled today saw great milestones being reached! It only gets better from here! Go josh...you got this...because HES GOT YOU!

—*Kristy OConnor*

Once Gwen and I knew about the timing of the surgery to reinstall Joshua's skull flaps, I made arrangements to travel to Houston. While we were blessed to have good BlueCross BlueShield insurance through my federal government job, we had to fund any additional travel and living expenses. We had already been blessed with donations to Joshua's GoFundMe page, which had been set up by our longtime friend Jeannette Balleza Collins, one of Joshua's mentors and the director of the ARK Challenge Accelerator that selected his first tech company for investment. In addition, we received many donations directly into a savings account that we had set up. Most of the largest donations were anonymous. Most of this money, so far, had been used to help with out-of-pocket medical expenses. We were now entering a phase with additional nonmedical expenses necessary to support Joshua's continued recovery. These costs were completely unknown at this point and could easily add up to tens of thousands of dollars.

Enter Jim Drake and Miracles for Mary. Patti Drake, Jim's wife, and Gwen had grown up together in Pine Bluff, Arkansas. They attended Catholic grade school and junior high together as well as the local public high school and then went their separate ways. I'd known Jim from our days coaching boys' basketball at our sons' respective Catholic elementary schools. Both of their boys were good players, and one was a scholarship player in college. Prior to Joshua's accident, I would characterize our relationship with the Drakes as cordial but not close.

The Drakes also had a daughter, Mary—also a talented student athlete at Mount Saint Mary Academy, an all-female Catholic school in the area, where she excelled in basketball. On the weekend before Thanksgiving in 2009, Mary and Blaine, her boyfriend at the time, were in a car accident. Several people were injured but none as bad as Mary. Every limb on her body was broken, and she suffered a severe head injury. Mary Drake was sixteen.

The Drakes would learn later that the EMTs who treated Mary at the crash site didn't think she would make it. She did, though. Today, Mary and the Drake family serve as examples for all of us who have gone through trials like this. Jim says, "You look back now and reflect on all the people that came and helped us—our support group and our church and our community—and you go wow, what do other people do if you don't have that? How are they getting through this?" That tough question was the driving force behind the Drakes' founding Miracles for Mary, a nonprofit that guides families through the transitions of a life-changing injury.

Unfortunately, sweet Mary Drake passed away in the spring of 2024 while in her late twenties. Miracles for Mary has provided more than $50,000 in support to families dealing with traumatic brain injuries and continues to operate and help survivors and their families.

While Joshua was still at UAMS in Little Rock, I received a call from Jim Drake. He said he and Patti knew what we were going through and wanted to help in any way they could. We met in the hospital cafeteria. We sat at a small table. I was still in my wheelchair. We talked, laughed, and prayed. I knew about their daughter Mary—nearly everyone in the Catholic community in central Arkansas did—but I knew nothing about Miracles for Mary. He offered to help with funding. At the time, early December, we didn't even know the extent of the current medical bills, let alone the expenses to come. I couldn't answer his question about what we needed, except for prayer. That was a given with Jim and Patti. They'd been praying for us since the day they heard about our accident.

Once it was apparent that Joshua was going to return to TIRR to begin his rehab, I calculated the travel expenses for me to fly to Houston several times. We had no idea how long Joshua would be in Houston, and I assumed that most of these flights could not be booked far enough in advance to get the lowest fares. I communicated the expense to Jim, minus what we could fund ourselves, and Miracles for Mary covered the rest. All Jim said was, "You'll have the money in your account in a few days. Let me know if you need more." We did eventually need more for rent and living expenses for Gwen and Joshua once he was discharged from TIRR. When I told Jim about those expenses, Miracles for Mary provided additional funding. What a blessing!

Joshua's custom skull flaps arrived, and he was scheduled for surgery the next day. Thank goodness that Gwen's sister Gloria and our friends the Davises were there. I arrived a few days later. I was looking forward to two hugs for Christmas. I couldn't have asked for a better gift.

The surgery to reinstall Joshua's skull flaps was successful, although it took an hour or more longer than anticipated. Why don't hospitals have beer taps or a bar in the waiting rooms? What a money maker! Sorry, my entrepreneurial mindset took over. The answer? Because there is a chapel on the first floor. Support trumps escape every time.

After the surgery, Joshua and Gwen rested as well as you can in a hospital, post-surgery. Joshua looked good but was still a bit groggy the next morning. We'd spent so many nights on a couch in a hospital that I'd made a few jokes about it. At one point, we had both been awakened around two o'clock in the morning by a few nurses checking on Joshua. In my semiconscious state, this whole scenario struck me as a bit humorous, and I turned to Gwen and said, "Who are these people in our bedroom?"

We both started laughing into our pillows so we wouldn't wake Joshua or make the nurses think we were laughing at them. As sleep-deprived as we were, even after all that, we snuggled up and went back to sleep.

The truth is, we felt very blessed that at least one of us had always been able to stay with Joshua in his room.

The day after Joshua's surgery at Memorial Hermann, physical therapists came in to start getting him moving. He'd been in bed for more than a month and lost thirty pounds. At nearly 6'4", he weighed only 130 pounds, had no muscle mass left, and was as weak as a kitten. Nevertheless, the PT staff was determined to get him moving. Gwen recalls that they were certainly no-nonsense. They got Joshua sitting up on the side of the bed, in a wheelchair, and standing. Gwen wasn't sure he was capable, and he wasn't always a willing participant, but he did it anyway. The female therapists were persistent and persuasive—persuasive like a Mafia version of persuasive, if you know what I mean. We appreciated that.

We were very thankful for God's healing hand in all this. We believed He guided the doctors and nurses and kept Joshua safe during the surgery. The medical staff told us the plan was to have him back over at TIRR's rehab facility in a few days. What a nice Christmas present that would be!

Only two days after Joshua's surgery, the doctor said he was ready for rehab at TIRR. This was another in a series of great examples from our experience that the healing hand of God is a mighty thing. We weren't sure when the move would happen, but it was a major milestone and a sign he was headed in the right direction.

Joshua still had some swelling from surgery, but he was looking good. He indicated several times that he wanted to shave his facial hair. Once that was done, he began to look like his old self again, except for the buzz cut.

While it was great being with Gwen and Joshua, we were missing someone very important. Our daughter, Emily, would be spending Christmas without her family for the first time. We asked everyone to please pray for her as well that Christmas season. She was feeling the stress of being away from her brother and family.

A CaringBridge response says it all:

> Hang in there Emily! Your family feels your love and they know you'd be there if you could. David, I'm so happy you are there with them. I know it's the only place you'd want to be right now. You are correct. The hand of Jesus is on Joshua and each of you. I'm praying for a peaceful and healing weekend. We are with you in prayers and thoughts.
>
> —*Sonya Coco*

On the afternoon of December 21, around four o'clock, the doctors cleared Joshua to return to TIRR. I rode with him in the ambulance. We settled in so he could rest after a long day of activity. Except for a bit of fever, he seemed to be doing okay. We prayed for a restful night and a Friday full of hope for a new beginning.

And so we returned to where we started when Joshua arrived in Houston. We were hopeful we'd get to stay for a while this time. Since his arrival at TIRR, we had experienced nine days of fear and uncertainty. Joshua had survived two brain surgeries and a potentially deadly episode with blood clots in his lungs. He'd been in the ER once and the ICU twice. Despite it all, I felt the great hope of a new adventure with God, and all of our friends and family, by our side.

We just prayed we weren't on a double roller coaster.

The Fog Begins to Clear

Joshua returned to TIRR the afternoon of December 21. Therapy began on the morning of December 22. They do not mess around at TIRR. As promised prior to Joshua's arrival, therapy wasn't just a few hours a day. It was a few hours per session, three sessions per day, six days per week, including speech, occupational, cognitive, and physical therapies. This is one of the reasons we chose TIRR—and why it is considered one of the top TBI and spinal-injury therapy facilities in the country.

It was good to see Dr. Kothari again. He is recognized globally as an expert in brain injury therapy. Dr. Kothari has been awarded the Humanitarian of the Year Award by the Texas Brain Injury Alliance for his work with the Rehabilitation Services Volunteer Project. The mother of Nick Tullier, the police officer shot in Baton Rouge who rehabbed at TIRR, calls him the "Brain Whisperer."

No rest for the weary. Joshua didn't sleep much his first night back at TIRR—a few hours at best. He was very active and kept trying to sit up. I talked to him about getting some rest so he'd be fresh when the therapists came in the next morning to start their assessments. I was concerned he'd be too tired to respond. He clearly had other things on his mind.

The next morning the doctors and therapists peppered Joshua with dozens of questions, which he answered with a thumbs-up for *yes* or thumbs-down for *no*. He was also asked to perform a number of physical actions as well. At one point the occupational therapist had him sitting in a wheelchair.

Gwen happened to not be in the room when Kayla, the speech therapist, arrived. She reminded me of Emily Anne, our great speech therapist from UAMS. Joshua answered every question that Kayla had for him, including his location, the date, where he was born (Texas), where he lived, and even a trick question about whether milk comes from cows. Okay, that wasn't exactly a trick question, but as Kayla explained, it was a question that required an understanding of a variety of things all in one question. He also wrote a zero on a whiteboard with his left hand. Finally, Kayla asked if he had his phone in the room. I found his iPhone, which had been in safekeeping since the accident, and handed it to him. It was locked, of course. Neither Gwen nor I knew his code, and he had been unable to tell us. We weren't sure we'd ever get into that phone again. Kayla asked him if he knew the code. I thought, *Yeah, right.* He didn't respond but started typing in numbers with his left hand. On the third try ... HE UNLOCKED THE PHONE!

Kayla's mouth dropped open as she turned and looked at me, wide-eyed. She did a good job of remaining calm. I, on the other hand, did not. I can't say I recall everything about that moment, but I do recall laughing, crying, hugging, and praising God. I knew, at that point, that our Joshua was in there!

For perspective, a little more than a week earlier, Joshua had arrived at TIRR with barely any command-response capability. On his first real day at TIRR, after a blood clot scare and two brain surgeries, he operated his iPhone. God is good, all the time.

As if that were not enough, that evening, when they returned Joshua from X-ray to his bed, he stumbled upon the TV controller, turned on the TV, changed channels until it stopped on a rerun of *Friends*, turned up the volume, and went to sleep.

WAY TO GO, JOSH!! I'm so proud of you. Keep up the good work!!

—*Emily Anne*

Praise the Lord! What wonderful news! I have never been so glad a kid could use his IPhone, it brought me to tears! I will continue to pray for more great days!

—*tara scallion*

While there was cause for celebration, we also knew that one good day did not guarantee a successful recovery.

We had already spent Thanksgiving in one hospital and now we would spend Christmas in another. Once again, we were missing our daughter and grandsons. While we missed all of the family, faith traditions, special foods, and familiar surroundings that would typically be part of Christmas, we felt incredibly blessed that we were all still here to spend Christmas together, no matter the conditions.

On Christmas Eve at TIRR, the staff was not on a normal schedule. Despite limited therapy, Joshua continued to improve little by little. He was up in his chair several times over those few days, gradually building his strength and regaining his range of motion, although total restoration was going to take months. He had lost so much weight and muscle mass that Gwen persisted in her recommendation to place him on a higher-calorie, higher-protein diet in conjunction with his muscle building therapy. He was also making progress toward getting off his trach. This was a multi-step process that we expected, at that point, would take a few weeks. Despite not speaking yet, Joshua had improved his ability to answer our questions by shaking his head slightly for *yes* or *no*.

While we never thought we'd ever spend a Christmas apart from our daughter, grandsons, and our extended families, the three of us were still alive and together, and that was a blessing. This could easily have been a Christmas without Joshua or me. Despite spending Christmas in a strange city, without our family and our Christmas traditions, it was the most special Christmas ever. We'd take blessings from God over presents any day.

Joshua's communication continued to improve. He could give Gwen and the nurses more information about how he was feeling and what he wanted. He no longer needed much help to get himself dressed for therapy each morning. He was also walking with a walker and needed little help to get himself in and out of a wheelchair.

We learned that Joshua had scar tissue on his larynx that was prohibiting him from talking. The solution was surgery—maybe several—to remove the scar tissue. That was disappointing news for Joshua. He displayed great frustration in his inability to communicate verbally. He routinely mouthed words in response to questions. Our concern was that the scar tissue would delay his trach removal by many weeks.

It was becoming clear that the greatest challenge of this journey might be the test of Joshua's patience and perseverance. He had always been able to achieve success by working harder and smarter. In this case, that was not enough. His body would only do what it was ready to do. Time and healing, two elements that none of us had any control over, were required for his recovery. Staying positive and encouraged was key. As he became more aware of his condition, he had to also confront that formidable challenge and figure out how to stay positive and continue to push himself.

My prayer continued to be for patience, perseverance, and God's healing hand.

Dear Moody family, My friend shared your story with us because our son suffered a TBI on July 1st. He has done very well in his recovery and will return to college. As we read your Caring Bridge entries our heart was touched by your recognition of God's goodness in this hardship. We have a "good, good Father" who knows just what you need. He is faithful to provide and He will. A verse that gave us peace when we were in rehabilitation is Psalms 139:5, "You hem me in, behind and before, and lay your hand upon me." We pray for your family to feel God's presence like never before! We rejoice that Josh has improved so much already! We make your prayer ours! God Bless You!

—*Dan, Gigi and Lee Parker*

This response to my CaringBridge journal was an example of several we received from people who had loved ones with a similar experience. In some cases, they were in the middle of the struggle just as we were. Sometimes, their loved ones had had a miraculous recovery, and in others the outcome was far less positive. These comments and connections were helpful and in some cases motivating.

All TBI cases are different due to the vast number of variables that can impact the health of the patient. As someone along the way told us, "If you've seen one TBI, you've seen one TBI."

Although we intentionally did not research the odds of survival and full recovery, we knew intuitively that they were not good. We tried hard not to be discouraged by the patient outcomes of the stories that were not so positive. We found comfort in the fact that their loved ones survived, that there were families out there to whom we could turn who knew exactly what we were going through, and that they cared enough to reach out to a family they didn't even know to offer their prayers and support.

Weekends typically involved less formal therapy. Joshua and Gwen had time to recoup and get out on their own. Gwen made sure they did that as often as possible. She asked for, and completed, training to handle certain elements of his care so that she could take him off the floor and, within reason, even out of the building.

Joshua and I started texting more often. It was amazing to me that he could do that just weeks following a TBI and multiple brain surgeries. I remember thinking, *Wow! Wow! Wow! God is good!*

It was during this time that we started to accumulate thousands of dollars in donations for Joshua. Several were anonymous, and I wanted to identify the first anonymous donor so that I could thank him or her. My banker, Mike Baldwin, a friend for many years, said, "We might be able to figure out who it is, but you just need to leave that alone, brother. Let them be anonymous if that's what they want." He was right, of course. We were simply thankful and feeling very blessed.

Gwen had been away from her teaching job for six weeks. With everything that was going on, we hadn't noticed that she was still receiving a paycheck every two weeks. Per her contract, she gets only a few weeks of personal and sick days, and by the time the accident occurred in November she had already used a few of them. As we found out later, her school family donated some of their leave days every pay period so that she could continue getting paid. No one told us; they just did it. This was another blessing that sustained us.

I suppose it goes without saying that we have great love in our hearts for the doctors, nurses, nursing techs, and therapists at TIRR. We had been blessed at UAMS with great doctors, nurses and therapists, and that certainly continued at TIRR. One of those great nurses was Jeff Bays. Although the nurses rotated, Jeff was with Joshua more than most. We were always so pleased when he was on duty. He talked to Joshua, even joked with him despite not always knowing if he was conscious enough to respond, was incredibly respectful while performing some unpleasant duties, and always listened to Gwen when she had questions or concerns.

Jeff recalls, "As an ER nurse, resuscitation and stabilization is your main focus. Young men are incredibly resilient, but we lost too many despite our best efforts. So when we would bring a young man back or stabilize somebody who rolled in with lights and sirens with little hope, we all felt incredibly thankful. I was naive at the time to what a long-term prognosis would often be or what length and intensity of rehab would be for these young men down the road."

Jeff eventually left Dallas for Austin and transitioned from the ER to a neuro step-down unit. In hospital lingo, that is where patients go when they leave the ICU. Jeff says that "I began to see the long-term recovery these young men would face. I also started to see the impact these injuries had on families. Sadly, it was in this setting that I realized so many of the young men I had helped save in the ER were now horribly cognitively impaired. The prognosis for some was bleak. Watching parents come to grips with that and the long-term ramifications was just as hard as losing a patient sometimes."

While in Austin, Jeff had helped patients transition from the trauma unit of the hospital to rehab at TIRR for many years. After relocating to Houston, on a whim, he sent a resume to TIRR. With no experience in rehab, he didn't believe he had much of a chance of landing the job. To his surprise, he got an offer to join the Brain Injury team, known as one of the best in the country for results with TBI patients. "At TIRR," Jeff says, "we often got a mix of patients, but I still had a soft spot for my young guys. My wife will tell you it's because I did so many dumb and dangerous things as a young man myself.

"My initial thought when I met Joshua was that he had some

good things going for him and at the same time, some things that could be HUGE potential problems. Joshua's head injury was bad but not the worst I had seen. He also wasn't what I would call a polytrauma patient. He had a TBI but hadn't been too badly mangled overall. It's hard enough recovering from a TBI, but adding amputations, multiple broken bones, respiratory failures, trachs, feeding tubes, etc. into a recovery just makes it so much harder.

"The downside to not being a polytrauma? Mobility and strength are retained but sometimes not important cognitive aspects. Some of my most difficult patients in my time at TIRR were young men with TBIs that had very poor ability to control emotions, impulse control, anger issues, manipulation, memory problems, and violent physical outbursts. If you will, imagine a three-year old child in the middle of a full-blown temper tantrum meltdown. Ok, make that three-year-old child, six foot, and 170 pounds."

Many years earlier, a trauma doctor had told Jeff that a person only needs three bones to survive: a wishbone, a backbone, and a funny bone. Jeff describes Joshua as "mostly aware of his deficits … He wasn't in complete denial and confused on why he was there. He wished to get better, and while that sounds so simple, it is the key to meaningful rehab. I've seen many patients who are either too cognitively impaired from the injury to be able to process why they are there or too severely depressed to engage and participate in therapies.

"He definitely had a backbone. He was a hard worker, and I remember his therapists had nothing but praise for him after their sessions. And lastly, he had his funny bone. One of my stronger memories of Joshua was a very positive sign. I use humor in my job for lots of reasons, but truthfully, I also feel like it's an important assessment tool. Humor takes brainpower, especially if it's not a simple knock-knock joke. Wordplay, timing, the ability to follow a storyline till the punchline, etc. I can't remember what exactly I said, but I deadpanned a lame joke. Josh got it and gave me a smirk. You won't find it in any medical journals or a clinical study about it, but I am convinced that humor is a valuable tool in seeing my patients progress and come out of the mental fog that happens with TBIs."

In some very kind comments directed at Gwen and me, Jeff says, "Joshua also had a HUGE advantage that is not discussed too openly by most hospitals. He had you guys. I cannot articulate how important active and involved family at the bedside is to recovery. My time at TIRR has shown it over and over. Patients with families that are at the bedside during their hospitalization do better. I've seen other young men with injuries similar to your son's with little or no family support. Their outcomes are poor, consistently. I realized early on talking with Gwen and you that Joshua had a family that was going to be exactly what he needed in his recovery. Supportive, patient, and able to read Joshua better than any nurse or therapist. You guys were great. You pushed him when he needed it and also gave him a rock to fall back on when I am sure he had fears and was worried about his recovery."

We thank God for putting Jeff in our path.

By the time we encountered Jeff he had been a nursing tech for three years and a nurse for twelve. He started in one of the largest ERs in the Dallas–Fort Worth area and worked his way up to their trauma team.

Joshua's progress was nothing short of amazing the first week of January. He was walking for short distances with only slight help from his occupational therapist, riding the stationary bike, and playing video games standing up. He was texting his friends and helping his mom figure out her phone features. He had been working hard each day through several hours of therapy, which also helped him sleep. He was able to go to Mass with Gwen twice that week.

Joshua was improving at such a pace that his doctors began to discuss a release date. It was possible that he only had a few weeks left at TIRR. They were as impressed with his recovery as we were. More important decisions lay ahead regarding outpatient therapy. While Joshua still had a long road ahead, his progress in just those few weeks was nothing short of miraculous.

> What a joy to be able to witness a miracle! God is great and fulfills His promises to those who are faithful. Thanks for giving us a front row seat!
>
> —*Mary Baskin*

> What incredible news. I literally cried while I read this post. The power of God's grace and mercy are inexhaustible. News like this gives us all hope. So happy that Josh was able to go to Mass. God is good. Love you guys. Paul
>
> —*Paul Wendel*

Joshua was doing well with swallow tests and began trying foods like applesauce. He was scheduled for a throat dilation, an outpatient procedure that we hoped would help him regain his voice. The procedure, scheduled on January 6, was not successful. The doctors didn't dilate at all because the scar tissue was too extensive. He would need surgery, and maybe more than one, to remove that scar tissue. The issue was that the scar tissue was impeding the flow of air through his vocal cords. We started gathering information to help us decide whether to have the surgery in Houston or UAMS. As it turned out, this was a somewhat specialized surgery requiring a week in the hospital for observation and recovery. Identifying a surgeon with extensive airway surgery experience was key to our decision.

Even though they didn't go through with the throat procedure, it required putting Joshua under a general anesthetic. He was still a bit groggy the next morning when I did a FaceTime call with him. No matter. He had a full day of therapy scheduled. As his occupational therapist would tell him, "You don't get stronger sitting in bed." We loved her approach.

It was disappointing for all of us, especially Joshua, but as Gwen said at the time, "I guess God isn't done with us yet." The surgery and recovery, and possibly multiple rounds of that, would take place over the next few months. This was certainly going to be yet another test of Joshua's patience. He was ready to speak and eat again. We were open to whatever might be coming our way at that point and knew that God, and all of the prayers we received from our friends and family, would ensure that we would have what we needed to get through it. In one of my CaringBridge posts at this time, I wrote, "We all have to remember that while we are focused on these short-term issues, his brain is slowly continuing to heal. What a blessing!"

Father West made a surprise visit following the throat dilation and stayed for one night and the following morning. He made the nine-hour drive just to see Joshua for a few hours. What a blessing he was for all of us. Joshua pushed through the effects of his anesthesia that night to visit with him for several hours. We were so thankful for his constant prayer and support.

This portion of my CaringBridge post on January 6 will give you a sense of our mindset at the time:

> We don't know what today will bring, but we have faith that it will further the miracle that we are all a part of and that, if there are setbacks, we will have the strength and patience to handle it.

Joshua continued to improve. Although he still had a PEG tube, a trach, and his eye misalignment, he began eating a variety of ground-up meats and vegetables. PEG is an acronym for Percutaneous Endoscopic Gastrostomy, a procedure in which a flexible feeding tube is placed through the abdominal wall and into the stomach. Joshua had been on a PEG tube since the accident. The consistency of food he was consuming orally at this point was generally that of mashed potatoes. If all went well, he could do another swallow test soon to see if he could move on to more solid foods. Nutrition served through the PEG tube was several small cartons of thick liquid—kind of like protein shakes—three times per day. These swallow tests were critical to his progress at this point. If he didn't continue to improve and pass these tests, he would remain on the PEG tube due to the possibility of choking or the food getting into his lungs and causing an infection.

One day Gwen sent me a video of Joshua walking up stairs and around obstacles, passing a basketball, and even jogging a little. His smile was coming back; he was grinning and shaking his head at my corny jokes—clearly a sign of advanced cognitive ability. I was planning to take his laptop to him on my next trip to Houston. I couldn't wait to see what would happen with that.

The doctors and caseworkers were still talking about releasing Joshua in ten days or so. We were waiting for information regarding options for his throat surgery, we hadn't decided where he would start his outpatient rehab, and Gwen and Joshua had no place to live. Once again, we were about to make a significant transition with only half of the information we needed to make decisions, with options for rehab, surgeries, and living accommodation that were unclear. We were discerning all this and praying about it.

Despite the uncertainty, those days were so different than the early dark days in mid-November. While it seemed like we had been on this journey quite a while (evidence that sleeping on a pullout bed in a hospital room for prolonged periods can affect your memory), it had only been two months. Joshua's progress from being semiconscious with minimal movement and communication to jogging, eating, and communicating in just two months—including three brain surgeries—was a miracle. Yet, as miraculous as it had already been, we were only in the first few chapters of a new book. I couldn't wait to see how God would write the rest of this story.

> I was one of Josh's nurses on H4 at UAMS. I am so ecstatic to see this positive update. Without a doubt, he is a miracle indeed! We often do not see miraculous outcomes like this. He is very blessed to have such supportive parents who never left his side and I'm sure prayed for him without ceasing.
>
> —*Natalie Svendsen*

Yes, we did, Natalie! Yes, we did.

In mid-January, after a busy week at work, I flew to Houston to visit Gwen and Joshua briefly over the weekend. I was using a cane at that point. That Friday night I got to hug my son standing up for the first time in two months. I can't express in words how wonderful that was. What a blessing!

It was still difficult for me to wrap my head around the reality that one month earlier Joshua had been in Memorial Hermann undergoing two brain surgeries to take fluid off his brain and put his skull flaps back in place. This was no doubt a miracle in progress, and I did my best to remind everyone who was following our story—all those who donated money and all those who prayed, called, and visited—that they were a part of the miracle.

We had a great visit that weekend. We shared meals, communicated on a whole host of subjects, got outside for a bit, and watched some playoff football. Joshua had progressed to a chopped food diet, which meant he could eat certain sandwiches, meats, veggies, and dessert as long as they were either soft or chopped into pieces. He enjoyed a hamburger while I was there. He walked much faster than I did down the hall as well. Gwen continued to get him taken off certain medications, if they were no longer needed, or switched to pill form so that he would be able to take them without his feeding tube. He was going to leave the hospital soon, and his medical care would be a bit easier on Gwen without the tube.

It was great to hug my beautiful wife as well. She was being so strong. God put her in this position to help Joshua. She was the right person for the job—just the right balance of patience, persistence, compassion, and push.

January 18 had become the target date for leaving TIRR. That both excited and terrified us. We had had great care there, and now that responsibility would fall to Joshua and Gwen. Living accommodations for Joshua and Gwen, Joshua's therapy location, and his pending throat surgery were all still up in the air. We hadn't decided whether we would be in Arkansas, Texas, or both. Other than that, we were in good shape and knew exactly what we were doing!

As I told Gwen that weekend, it would all fall into place. She sent me a graphic after I returned home that read, *If God brings you to it, He will bring you through it.* We were letting our faith lead us, and we believed that one hundred percent. When we began to overthink it, we began to worry and doubt the outcome. We prayed every day to stay strong, to let God lead us, and to do our best. Everything else would take care of itself.

The next few days were filled with visits to potential apartments in Houston and the potential therapy locations we identified, conversations with throat surgeons in both Houston and Little Rock, and conversations with potential therapy locations in Arkansas. Regarding those, we were concerned that Joshua was now overqualified for one and underqualified for the other. As always, it was all about what would yield the most thorough, fastest recovery.

One challenge that was always on our minds was money. The possibility of paying for living accommodations in Houston for a few months was just another one. Once again, we tried to not worry and continued to believe that God would lead us and provide a path. We had been incredibly blessed with donations.

We were able to arrange just a few more days at TIRR. We needed the extra time, hoping that things would fall into place. As we moved past the original discharge date, Joshua continued to improve. He continued to push himself with physical therapy. In my tweets and FaceTime calls, I could see our Joshua gradually coming back. Gwen continued to be strong and was very busy securing doctor appointments and temporary housing.

An appointment with a surgeon at Baylor College of Medicine helped us decide in favor of Houston for Joshua's scar tissue surgery. We were thinking that if we had the surgery done soon in Houston with this doctor, Joshua would likely continue his therapy in TIRR's outpatient program. If the surgery could not be scheduled soon in Houston, we would consider returning home to have the surgery at UAMS. We had prayers and guidance and help from the medical staffs at TIRR and UAMS to help us discern what to do. We felt strongly that God had led us to this point and that He would continue to push us forward.

Gwen and Joshua were ready to return home, and Emily and I were so ready to have us all back together. But this surgery was critical to his ability to speak, and we wanted the best possible option available to him.

While all this was going on in Houston, I had a small army of people taking care of me in Arkansas. Family, church folks, and old friends (Donna Nichols, Jane Tiefel, Linda Bridges, and John Stewart, just to name a few) volunteered to bring meals and transport me to and from work and physical therapy while I was waiting to be cleared to drive.

As my old friend Max was fond of saying, "God had blessed us in a MIGHTY way!"

The Whisper Was a ROAR

Joshua and Gwen left TIRR the last week of January, with an emotional walk down the hall to the elevator, as is the tradition. As you may imagine, tears were flowing, and hugs were abundant and heartfelt. The staff had become an extended family for Gwen and Joshua for a month. They took care of Joshua, and in return we cared about them. As we had done with the staff at UAMS, we promised to return and thank them properly someday. While we were happy that Joshua was able to leave due to his incredible progress, we were very nervous about leaving the good care he received at TIRR.

In the weeks leading up to their departure from TIRR, Gwen had been busy trying to figure out where she and Joshua could live. They needed to be reasonably close to the surgeons and hospitals where future surgeries might occur. We had no idea how long Gwen and Joshua would be there, and since these living expenses were not covered by insurance, the cost was a big concern. As fate would have it, Gwen's sister Gloria and her husband, Pierre, were well connected in the apartment management industry in Texas. Gloria had managed apartments earlier in her career, and Pierre was the VP of Sales for a large, locally owned carpet distribution and installation company that catered to the apartment management companies in Houston, Dallas, San Antonio, and Austin. Although Gloria was not employed in the industry anymore, they were both very active in state and national apartment management associations. During Gwen's apartment search, Gloria connected her to a friend, John Ridgeway, who had recently purchased an apartment complex just a few blocks from the Houston medical district.

The Texas Medical Center (TMC) is more of a complex than a particular location. It is an amazing place. According to their website, the TMC is the largest medical complex in the world and home to the world's largest children's hospital and world's largest cancer hospital.

Gloria's apartment connection turned out to be another gift from God. The new owner intended to remodel and update the complex and eventually sell it. He offered Gwen a below-market rate and an arrangement whereby Joshua and Gwen would be able to live in a two-bedroom apartment with the understanding they might be asked to move around a bit as the apartments were remodeled. The location was perfect. Joshua and Gwen left TIRR and moved in that day.

Since Gwen and Joshua had been living in hospital rooms for two months, they traveled fairly light with just two suitcases and a few small bags. They moved into their apartment, staked out their bedrooms, and began to put things away and settle in. It had been a long day, so they both decided to take an afternoon nap.

In the late afternoon, Joshua woke up. He reached for his cannula to clean his trach. When he took the cap off, he coughed hard, and his trach came completely out of his throat. He scrambled to replace it but couldn't. It only took a few seconds for his breathing to become labored as the opening in his throat slowly closed. Concerned about exerting himself and making his breathing issues even worse, he reached for his phone and called Gwen from his bed.

Gwen was asleep in her bedroom when the ringing phone woke her up. Coming out of a deep sleep, at first she was confused as to who was calling her. Joshua couldn't speak. After a few seconds, she realized what was going on and leaped out of her bed and down the hallway to Joshua's room. When she arrived, she saw Joshua in his bed, laboring to breathe, with his trach tube lying beside him on the bed. Gwen called 911 and the apartment manager.

The ambulance took Joshua to the ER at Memorial Hermann. The ER staff replaced his trach and cannula. Gwen called me, and we discussed the situation. She was upset and concerned that the replacement cannula the ER staff used was the incorrect size and that they might end up back in the ER in the middle of the night. The ER staff was ready to send Joshua home, but after our call Gwen insisted he stay the night for observation. She and Joshua needed to be in a safe place. Before he was released the next day, the speech therapist had inserted the proper size cannula. Once again, Gwen's quick thinking and persistence influenced a critical outcome.

The incident scared both of them. Joshua's miraculous progress could make it easy for us to lose sight of the facts that his injury was deadly serious, that he still had a trach and surgeries ahead, and that we were on the front end of a long journey to recovery, with God at our side.

Thus began the next chapter of Joshua's recovery. The pace would now shift from scary incidents and miraculous improvements every week to waiting on appointments and tracking incremental progress. We had to make that shift mentally. While Gwen and I were ready for fewer emergencies and less frequent life-changing decisions, this period tested our patience.

In the days following the trach incident, Joshua and Gwen, with the help of our dear friend Robin, traveled to three surgeon appointments. We were hopeful that the information gained from these visits would give us the insight we needed to make decisions about surgery and the path forward. These next few months would be filled with major milestones in Joshua's recovery.

That must have been so frightening for them. Whew! It's
been a rough journey. There is definitely a light at the end
of this tunnel: his full recovery. Our God is a Mighty God!

—Elizabeth Roberts

Joshua was at a critical point in his recovery. The initial surgery to remove scar tissue from his airway was scheduled for January 31. The surgery was outpatient with a follow-up visit in three weeks. Joshua and Gwen remained in their Houston apartment during that time since it was closer to follow-up care if needed.

Several types of surgeries can remedy this condition, known as subglottic stenosis, a narrowing of the subglottis (the area of the windpipe just below the vocal folds). The surgeries range from using dilation and a balloon to widen the airway, to cutting away the scar tissue, to removing the section of the trachea that contains the scar tissue and sewing the trachea back together. The source of this condition was likely the breathing tube placed in Joshua's throat when he was admitted to UAMS in an unconscious state, two weeks before his tracheotomy. No matter the surgical type, all were serious surgeries with no guarantee that Joshua's voice would be restored or that his trach tube would eventually be removed.

Gwen, Joshua, and I had been apart for six weeks, except for a few brief visits, and the lack of access to family and friends was definitely a challenge for them. Due to my inability to drive, we had not seen our grandsons since mid-December, and I'd only seen our daughter, Emily, twice since November. We depended on each other for support, and this was yet one more challenge for us.

For me, the void I felt without my family had been filled, to a degree, by an outpouring of love and support. Our friend Chris Herrings took me to our Men of Faith group and to Mass. Mass was emotional for me in those days as I considered how blessed we were to all still be here and that

Joshua's recovery so far had been a miracle. It's common to grow closer to God during times of strife. The challenge for all of us would be to keep this special feeling when our hour of need had passed and we returned to the world. I prayed that our faith would stay strong.

Despite the uncertainty of surgery and the lack of access to family, we believed God had brought us this far along the journey and that He would bring us the rest of the way home. It might not be easy, and things might not happen on the timeline we'd prefer, but we couldn't control any of that, so we put it all in His hands. In business we say that if you trust the process then you can't question the outcome. We trusted God's process. We believed the outcome, although unknown, could lead us somewhere very special. We chose to embrace the journey.

> Dave, I truly thank you for sharing this journey that you, Gwen, and Joshua have been on. To love and pray with you through the lows and to celebrate the triumphs and true miracles with you has been, and continues to be, a privilege. We love you and we thank God for you! Thank you for giving us direction in our prayers for you and Josh!
>
> —*Kathy Wendel*

> We are praying for you all everyday. God has Joshua all wrapped up in His love and is taking great care of him through his amazing parents and the expert medical care he is receiving. Thank you for your updates that keep us informed and shine God's grace so brightly. Wednesday is a big day and one that we look forward to God's healing through a successful surgery. Y'all are going to get to visit those grandsons soon, and they will someday marvel at today's miracle in your family!!!
>
> —*mindy gibbons*

... God's timing is perfect. I will pray that Joshua will be at peace. Deuteronomy 31 tells us about Moses instructing the Israelites before they crossed into the Promised Land. Verse 3, "The Lord himself will cross over ahead of you ..." Verse 6, "Be strong and courageous. Do not be afraid for the Lord your God goes with you; he will never leave you nor forsake you."

The Lord himself is moving ahead preparing great things for Joshua and your family.

—*Gigi Parker*

Surgery to begin removing the scar tissue from Joshua's trachea was rescheduled for February 2. We asked all of our friends, family, and church family for their prayers that day. As it turned out, Joshua's surgery was being performed in a Catholic hospital on the feast day of St. Blaise, when we traditionally have the blessing of the throat. St. Blaise miraculously restored a little child who was at the point of death because of an affliction of the throat.

Despite great doctors and lots of prayer, the surgery to remove the scar tissue from Joshua's trachea was unsuccessful. He still had his trach tube and no voice. This could have felt like a setback, but it wasn't. We were mentally prepared for this result.

We were hopeful that the surgeon could schedule Joshua's next surgery very soon. That surgery would be a tracheal resection, in which the surgeon removes the section of his trachea with thick scar tissue and then sews the trachea back together. This would, we hoped, get his trach tube out and his voice back. We were one step closer to recovery, and we were confident that we had a plan and the right surgeons to get us there.

◆

Gwen and Joshua settled into apartment life. The apartment had two bedrooms with a kitchen, dining area, living room, and small back patio.

The complex was located in a cluster of other apartment complexes. Within walking distance were a Walgreens, fast food restaurants, a doughnut shop, and a grocery store. Gwen did not have a car in Houston. Every few days, she would push Joshua in his wheelchair—he was too weak to walk very far with good balance—to get groceries, doughnuts, or fast food. Typically, they returned with Gwen pushing a wheelchair with bags of groceries stacked in Joshua's lap and hanging from any part of the chair that would hold them.

During this period, Gwen commented in one of our phone calls that she no longer dreamed while she slept. Gwen had always had vivid dreams—so vivid, in fact, that she might wake up angry with me for something I'd done in her dream. I have a hard enough time trying to defend the stupid stuff I actually do! Gwen believed this was a gift from God to help her cope with the trauma she was dealing with. She had seen her beloved son in dire circumstances and near death several times by this point. If she had to relive those events in her dreams, it would further traumatize her and keep her from getting the rest she desperately needed to be on top of her game as a full-time caregiver.

In the weeks between surgeries, Joshua spent his days maintaining his health and trying to exercise a bit, do a little work on the computer, and play some video games. He was pleased when a cognitive therapist at TIRR told him that video games would be good for his brain recovery. He certainly had never heard that from his parents.

During this time, Gwen arranged for continued therapy for Joshua with an organization called Rehab Without Walls (RWW). Highly qualified therapists came to the apartment weekly to help with occupational and physical therapy. They were wonderful! They helped Joshua work on his balance and coordination, regain his mental capacity for planning and organization, and execute basic life skills. This included tasks such as solving puzzles and going to the grocery store. The sessions were typically three to four times per week, four hours per day, on days when he didn't have a doctor's appointment. It's unfortunate that every region of the country doesn't have such accessible, highly qualified therapists who are covered by insurance. Joshua generally had the same two or three therapists during his time in the apartment. Both Joshua and Gwen formed relationships with these young therapists. Some of them enjoyed Joshua's quick wit and sometimes quirky sense of humor. They also served as sources of medical guidance and outlets for conversation for Gwen, both of which she needed.

Nothing happened as quickly as we wanted during this phase of Joshua's recovery. The miraculous advances we witnessed every week at TIRR were now coming in small increments weeks apart. It was nearly two weeks before we could schedule his next trachea surgery. The procedure would require a week in the hospital for observation of his airway. The surgeon was confident in a positive outcome, and we were confident in him and his team. If the surgery was successful, Joshua would get his voice back and his trach out. It was also possible that, even with clearing out the scar tissue, his voice mechanics would still not work.

In mid-February I flew back to Houston for the surgery. Joshua was a bit nervous, as we all were. It was major surgery which, by its very nature, entails risk. Complications could cause him to have to live the rest of his life with a trach. We were told that the procedure could result in additional scar tissue growth and require further treatment. To put this in perspective, however, Joshua had already undergone several emergency surgeries since the accident that were unplanned, high risk, and had unknown, possibly life-threatening outcomes.

Dr. Shawn S. Groth, a general thoracic surgeon specializing in minimally invasive esophageal surgery, scheduled the early morning surgery for February 13th. One of us was allowed to accompany Joshua into surgery prep that morning. We all knew who that was going to be, and it wasn't me. Gwen was Joshua's mother and patient advocate. We were so blessed she was able to be with him on this journey. This was my CaringBridge post from the waiting room that morning:

> I'm thinking about all the love and prayers you all send our way. It feels so good. Like a warm blanket. Which, by the way, I wish I was still under. We've been up for several hours already. Please keep the surgical team in your prayers this morning, as well as Joshua. Also, pray that we all have the peace and grace to handle whatever comes next. God is good, all the time. More later.

During the surgery we received updates from the surgical nurse. The updates indicated that everything was going well, but there was never much detail. I was thinking to myself, *It's major surgery. Everything can be going well, until it's not.* We had experienced that multiple times on this journey.

Five hours in, we were told that the surgery had gone well so far, that the section of scar tissue in his trachea had been removed, and there was still hope that they would not need to put a trach tube back in. Finally, Gwen and I were told that the surgery was finished and that the doctor would meet us in a side room to give us the details. Dr. Groth told us that Joshua's surgery was successful. The scar tissue had been removed, as had his trach tube. He would have a breathing tube overnight as a precaution. We would not know about his voice for another few days.

Sometime after surgery, I wrote a post on CaringBridge to inform everyone of the outcome. These were my final thoughts in that post:

> While it has been a long day, it has been made far more peaceful than stressful because of the presence of the Holy Spirit and the love, prayers and support from each of you.

> God truly had His healing hand on Joshua and the surgical team today. The miracle continues …

Joshua was placed in ICU to recover. The surgeon had inserted an anchor stitch, a thick suture attached under his chin and upper chest. It kept him from moving his head too far back and reopening the incision in his throat. It looked strange, and it felt strange to Joshua, but it worked. We were told it would come out once the stitches in his throat had done their job.

It was Valentine's Day, the day after the tracheal resection, when we first met Kristi Vidaurri Foley, a speech pathologist with CHI St. Luke's Health at Baylor St. Luke's Medical Center. The doctors had just left Joshua's room in the ICU and, as was normal during these brief visits, left several questions unanswered regarding what to expect. In typical Gwen fashion, she approached the nurse's station seeking answers.

Kristi recalled, "I remember sitting at a computer in the ICU at St. Luke's Hospital, talking with some nurses about another patient, when Gwen walked up to the desk asking to speak with the nurse. When she walked up to the nurse's station, I remember she appeared nervous and anxious, fidgeting her hands like she didn't want to bother anyone but had some questions about what the doctor just said. I guess they had just left Joshua's room.

"I was curious and nosy, so I took a peek into the room that Gwen walked into, and I remember seeing Josh sitting in a chair, staring forward, with the anchor stitch from his chin to his chest. He looked like a kid, well, he kinda was. I thought to myself, *What is he doing here?*"

Kristi remembered asking the nurse practitioner about him. The nurse practitioner responded, "Don't worry, you will know all about him since you will see him tomorrow." Kristi thought, *Oh great, a kid transferred from another hospital or rehab because somebody screwed something up somewhere, and he is here for some radical procedure or infection.* She then realized why Gwen appeared to be so anxious. She also recalled that Gwen, while anxious, was not frantic. Kristi got the feeling that Gwen had done this hospital thing for a while.

"So, there I was the next morning," recalls Kristi, "reviewing this young patient's chart and getting a CliffsNotes version of his history and reason for admission. I heard *tracheal resection*, and I asked again, thinking that I misunderstood what the nurse practitioner had said. She repeated 'tracheal resection' so nonchalantly, like it was some mundane, benign procedure. I didn't ask much else because I wanted to read the narrative leading up to this procedure. Mind you, I had never seen a tracheal resection that resulted in restoration of normal function. I had only heard of or seen this procedure done at the VA when I was in graduate school in a 'we don't have any other option' type of situation, usually due to tumors."

Kristi didn't divulge this at the time, but she read in the notes that some ear, nose, and throat doctors said that Joshua likely wouldn't speak again, or at least for an undetermined period of time, due to the degree of stenosis, or narrowing in his trachea after multiple intubations. She remembers thinking, "What the hell am I supposed to do with this kid? He had just had three centimeters of his trachea cut out of his throat and then stitched back together approximately twenty-four hours prior to me entering his room. All I know is that this kid came in with a T-trach to keep his trachea from collapsing."

Kristi had heard that Joshua had not spoken or made any type of sound with his voice since November, when the accident occurred. As she prepared to enter his ICU room, she thought to herself, *Kristi, please don't screw this up.*

"When I walked into the room," she recalls, "Gwen was standing and pacing. Again, I thought, *Don't screw this up and don't let them know you have never treated a fresh tracheal resection in your career.* As I usually do with strange or complex cases, I walked in and acted as if I saw this every day, as if it was no big deal. I attempted to explain the general therapy plan for speech and swallowing, including my role, as concisely as possible."

Although we didn't detect it at the time, Kristi said, "In reality I had knots inside my stomach … I am talking to a mother whose kid has gone through all this, if I screw it up, she will kill me."

She asked if Josh had spoken since the procedure. The nurse stated that the doctor recommended no sound or talking until a speech therapist was at his bedside. "So, here we were," Kristi remembers, "this kid who hadn't spoken in months, his very anxious mother, and no safety net, meaning no trach and only a few liters of oxygen. I made sure respiratory therapy was nearby before I did anything." She asked Josh to perform a few simple voicing exercises.

For the first time in months, Joshua made a sound with his voice and whispered his name.

For all of us, that whisper was a ROAR! For us it was a major milestone on this long road of recovery. After months of surgeries and therapy, Joshua could walk, he could think, and now he could speak.

Kristi recalls this moment vividly. "I remember the sweet smile Josh had on his face, followed by his 'no big deal' demeanor, which I figured out is his usual. Everyone gasped and cheered. Gwen cried. It was amazing, and I looked like a genius! This was one of those 'drop the mic' moments."

This was why Gwen and Joshua had stayed in Houston all those months. This was why we sacrificed being together. This was why Gwen gave up her teaching career and her school family and endured feelings of loneliness, many hours of worry, and the challenges and pressures of being Joshua's 24/7 caregiver.

Following Joshua's first words, my post on CaringBridge expressed our tremendous gratitude to friends and family for all the prayers and encouragement. As you can imagine, we received many, many responses. These are a few of them:

YAY FOR WHISPERS!! This speech therapist is over the moon!!! Keep up the good work, Josh!! :)

—*Emily Anne*

What an awesome Valentine's Day and first day of Lent gift for you all!

—*Debra and Joe Villiger*

Praise the Lord. Your family's faith is a beautiful testimony to what the Good Lord can do to heal emotionally and physically those that are suffering.

—*Kelly-Rawls Taylor*

Praise God for all He's done for Joshua and family. I'm not sure how anyone's faith couldn't be stronger. This is a miracle! Josh has a second chance at life. He has been blessed and so have we all. I'm so happy for you all. Continued prayers.

—*Sonya Coco*

It made my heart happy to hear him talk today. He was so happy today.

—*Robin Davis*

Who knew a whisper could be so loud.

—*Mary Baskin*

As is generally true of recovery, everything is a process. Removing the scar tissue and the recovery of Joshua's voice were major milestones.

However, we didn't know if his voice would return to normal or even improve, and his swallow mechanics had to improve so he could get his feeding tube removed. As it turns out, something most all of us take for granted—swallow mechanics—is fairly complex.

After a few days in ICU, Joshua was moved into a standard room. He was making good progress, with his surgery incision healing nicely and his voice getting stronger each day. He had started reciting movie lines since his voice had the low tone and raspy quality of Batman. I wondered how that might change over time, or if it would. He was not on a regular diet due to a lack of strength in his swallow mechanics. We expected that to improve over time so he could get back on his higher-calorie diet. He still had quite a bit of weight and muscle to regain.

Joshua's eyesight also continued to improve. He had been wearing an eye patch for a while at that point to help correct and strengthen the vision in his left eye. As his eyesight improved, he wasn't wearing his eye patch as often. He was growing a bit tired of the pirate references and looking forward to getting rid of the patch altogether—although the eye patch and Batman voice had been fun for a little while.

> Pirate and Batman!!!! Nothing wrong with this after all he's been through. Angels are all around him. Continued prayers for a special young man. I believe without a doubt God is using him to reach others. May each day be better than the day before. Jesus always and forever.
>
> —Sonya Coco

> Okay, I giggled out loud at the movie lines—of course he'd do that! That boy!!!!
>
> —Karen Boone

"Now," Kristi recalls, "I had to make sure he could swallow with this new go-go gadget trachea and not let anything go into his lungs."

Even though Joshua had been eating solid food with his trach tube in, now that it was out, there was a danger that food could get into his lungs until he learned to swallow again.

"Knowing anatomy, physiology, and lack of reflexive nerve sensation post resection," Kristi recalls, "I did something sweet Sugarplum did not like ... I took away his food. The plan was to give it back slowly as he could show me that his swallow function had returned."

Sugarplum was what Kristi started calling Joshua early on. As Gwen recalls, "While Kristi was serious about her work, she was very engaging with Joshua and had a great sense of humor. One day when she was telling him, in her matter-of-fact manner, how things were going to be and what he needed to do to recover, she referred to him as 'Sugarplum.' The name stuck and became a source of humor for all of us."

Joshua left the hospital on February 24th. Once again, he had bounced back quickly after a major surgery.

───◆───

While most of Joshua's surgeries had been emergencies with uncertain outcomes, this recent surgery went as planned and would have a major impact on his quality of life. His voice was back, his trach tube was out, he was almost back to a normal diet, and he had a cool scar on his throat, which I was certain would be the inspiration for any number of completely made-up stories as to how he got it. In fact, he had several new scars, most of which would not be visible. For me, those scars symbolize trauma and triumph for all of us. I hoped that in the future, each time he ran his fingers through his hair, buttoned the top buttons on his shirt, or patted his stomach after a great meal, he would think about what he came through and say a prayer of thanks for his many blessings.

Joshua eventually convinced Gwen that he was capable of making trips to nearby shops on his own, on foot. It was the highlight of his day to be out on his own for a bit. Gwen knew he needed to do this to regain his strength but still worried about him any time he was not with her. Whenever Joshua—who was still very skinny, unbalanced at times, and sporting an eye patch—would leave, Gwen would say, "Stand tall and walk with purpose," fearing someone might try to take advantage or harm him if he appeared weak. As Joshua strolled onto the sidewalk on his way to Smash Burger he would turn toward Gwen, smile, and say, "I'm walking with purpose, Momma."

During one of my visits, Joshua and I decided to go to the doughnut shop that served made-to-order doughnuts with dozens of uncommon toppings such as German chocolate or pralines and caramel. I was walking with a cane at this point. We walked to the shop and enjoyed our doughnuts, which were the size of a salad plate and very expensive. On our way home we walked slowly between apartment complexes, crossing streets and stepping over curbs to get onto sidewalks. At one point, the uneven terrain proved a bit much for us, and we both lost our balance but didn't fall. We looked at each other and both started laughing so hard that we had to stop for a moment. We knew how silly we looked. I said, "Boy, nobody's gonna mess with us," and Joshua replied, "We look like we came into town with the circus." There was a lot going on in our lives, but we had not lost our sense of humor. That was one of the many things that kept us going.

Two ways that we could tell that Joshua was on the mend were that he had his sense of humor thoroughly intact and that he still hated doing chores. During one of my visits to Houston, I asked him to take out the trash. His response was to flutter his eyelashes and say, "I can't … I'm on medication." We both got a big laugh out of that before I said, "Nice try, buddy." He still took out the trash.

I've spent a fair amount of my career making plans and executing them in government, nonprofits, and business organizations. We had no plan, however, for the first few stages of Joshua's recovery. He was totally in the hands of God and the medical team. Now, with God still by our side, he was moving through the outpatient phase of his rehab.

At this point, we were hoping for a return home before the end of March. Emily and I couldn't wait, and neither could Chippie—our cat who loved his momma but didn't always like me. (I have the scars to prove it!) We planned for Joshua to continue rehab once he returned home and anticipated that this next phase of recovery would likely be long, with incremental progress. As we had done the entire journey, we would seek the most aggressive, cutting-edge rehab available with the goal of helping Joshua be the best he could be as soon as possible.

As we entered this new phase of recovery, I hoped we would never forget the grace and healing power of God. Only our willingness to turn this over to Him had gotten us through those first few months in the hospital. The people He put in our path, the relationships with friends and family that had been rekindled, the kindness of our family, friends, and employers, and the medical staff that cared for Joshua had all been tremendous blessings. As we returned to a more normal life at home, I hoped we could maintain our complete trust in God, our newfound patience, and our feelings of thankfulness and humility. We knew that the world wouldn't make that an easy task. I hoped we were strong enough and guessed we would need to pray for that as well.

Glory be to God!

—Karen Boone

Beautiful writing as you share your thoughts, feelings, and gratefulness for God's Grace. WooHoo!! I'm so happy for you all! Love, Beth

—Elizabeth Roberts

Absolutely incredible!!!!

The whole Moody family are def saints on earth. God has blessed all of us who know this special family. They have shown us what it truly means to have faith beyond measure, love to no end, and how powerful his love is and he can do anything! Each one of you has a story to tell everyone that can change peoples lives for the better. I am so happy everything is going so well and I cannot wait till Joshua and Gwen are home! David, your words of encouragement and strength, from the very first post, have truly touched so many people. I know at times it was probably hard to write, but your attitude and strength got everyone through this trying time. You are definitely blessed with a miraculous gift and I hope that we can continue to give back to you guys during this recovery stage as much as you have given to us. GOD IS GOOD! ALL THE TIME!!

—Stephanie Gandolph

I am beyond thrilled to see the progress that Joshua has made. God has certainly had His hand in this. May we all continue to thank Him daily for our blessings. Prayers continue for you all as you continue to heal and get back to your life. Love and prayers!

—Sandra Starnes

My goodness this is such an inspiring post. I am literally in tears with joy reading about miracles that continue to happen along this journey. I can remember back to the time we were visiting while Josh was still at UAMS and demonstrating only limited responses. And then the priest from the Little Rock diocese that experienced the Traumatic brain (Fr Joseph Chan) injury came by and gave Josh a blessing and told you and Gwen that Josh would make a full recovery. I am amazed by his faith and prediction. God is good all the time. We love you and Gwen and Josh and look forward to the day when we can get together and share a glass of wine and some hugs and some laughs.

—Paul Wendel

You all are going to make it. Remember the road has been a pretty long one so far. And God has been with you all, every minute. Another thing you all still have so many prayers being lifted. I can't wait to see Joshua because he is a miracle. Jesus has plans for him. I pray that Joshua can make a wonderful difference in youth his age. I pray they see that Joshua is here because of the prayers from believers in Jesus Christ! I pray that many that have followed your posts now will give their lives to Jesus and follow HIM!! Jesus loves you!!

—Sonya Coco

Joshua and I were talking just this week about you and Chippie and how Chippie will be glad to see Gwen when they return home.

—Robin Davis

So thankful for Joshua's progress! The gift of healing from a gracious God! Thank you for sharing your journey!

—Gigi Parker

So happy for all of you. God is so good. Thank you for keeping us informed. Your courage, your strong faith, and your love for one another is such an inspiration. Thank you for all you mean to me.

—*Ruth Roberts*

It took several weeks and a few swallow tests with Kristi for Joshua to be cleared. Gwen was a nervous wreck during this period because Joshua wanted to eat everything in sight, even though his diet was restricted. She was constantly reminding him of the dangers of not following the diet restrictions and swallow protocols. At one point, she asked Kristi to reiterate the rules for consuming thick liquids and other foods to Josh. She knew Joshua would listen to Kristi and that she would be very matter of fact with him.

Kristi relates, "The last swallow test, the big finale that cleared him for regular food and thin liquid, was amazing. Fun Aunt was here"—Gwen's sister Gloria—"so she and Gwen both watched the test. When the X-ray machine turned off, us girls were so excited about the results. And there was Josh, looking at us like we were crazy. I know he was so excited but wanted to be super macho."

The next step was to get the feeding tube taken out. "Josh was a bit frail, like runway frail," Kristi says. "I told him he needed to fatten up for the winter. Again, he looked at me like I was crazy. I LOVED to tease him a bit."

The removal of the feeding tube was successful. By mid-March we were most thankful that Joshua had moved from survival to rehab mode. While he was not out of the woods yet regarding the scar tissue in his trachea, he was no longer in a life-threatening situation on a weekly basis. Scar tissue buildup from a tracheal resection surgery was still a possibility, so he underwent a few minor procedures to address that in the months following his major surgery.

In addition to the potential for scar tissue, Joshua still had an issue with his left eye. It was misaligned and caused his vision, which had been 20/20 prior to the accident, to be blurry. The doctors thought this condition, called strabismus, might realign itself as his brain healed. It hadn't yet. Since this was not life threatening, we decided to give it a bit more time to heal. If surgery was ultimately necessary, it would likely be done in Arkansas.

The time apart continued to impact all of us. Gwen had been incredibly strong, but the isolation and pressure of being Joshua's only caregiver 24/7, day in and day out, was wearing on her. While she wouldn't have been anywhere else but caring for him, she missed our little house, watching her flowers grow, playing with her grandsons, having a glass of wine with me on the deck, sleeping in her comfy bed, caring for her mom and dad, interacting with her school family—and of course, her precious students. Her life had been turned upside down in an instant … by me.

Now we had to begin to consider Joshua's future. While he had risked death several times and survived, his future was fraught with uncertainty even then. He would likely need a year, or maybe several years, of therapy with no guarantee of a return to the life he had before the accident. The cost of long-term therapy—and his ability to function normally, earn a living, and pursue his dreams—were all unknown at that point. Given this uncertainty, we had to continue to willingly hand it all over to God, try to not worry about it too much, and let His will be done.

> Thank you for the update. Praise God for all the many miracles and blessings that have come forward. God carrying all of you in the palm of His hand. Continue to speak healing words to Joshua for God is greater than any of it all, bringing forth all that is needed for all involved. God bless knowing that even in distance all are connected in the awesome peace of the Lord.
>
> —Marjo Hadfield

Thank you for the update. It sounds trite to say "If God leads you to it, He will lead you through it"—but I do believe that. I am praying it is so everyday for all of you!

—*Paige Smith*

We are so thankful that Josh is making such wonderful progress. We are thankful that each step has been taken with Jesus guiding him through it all. We know He has given each of you the strength to get through all of this. The unknown is always a bit uncomfortable but just know your family has many prayer warriors helps with each step. We don't know why this happened, but we sure know WHO has been right there to see you all through. May God continue to be all you need. Give Gwen our love. Our walk in life is with Jesus!!! I hope your therapy has gone good for you and you have recovered well too.

—*Sonya Coco*

David, Gwen, and Joshua, you all continue to be in my prayers as well as Emily and your grandsons. I know this has been a most challenging time for all of you. Your faith is so strong. I continue to be blessed hearing the progress Joshua is making.

Special prayers for Gwen being a caregiver.

David, I hope your rehab is going well and you are getting stronger every day, mentally and physically. I know you would like to be with Gwen and Joshua during his time of rehab. God is with you all. May He continue to comfort and bless you. Love and prayers, Paula

—*Paula Findley*

On April 1, Easter Sunday, Gwen, Joshua and I spent time together in our own home for the first time in almost five months. They were able to fly home for the weekend. Words can't express what a blessing that was for all of us. It was not lost on us that this opportunity took place during Easter week. The timing accentuated the feelings of loss, hope, renewal, trust in promises made, and the power of our Almighty God that Christians experience each Easter.

The opportunity for Gwen and Joshua to fly home at the last minute was made possible by Gwen's sister Gloria, her husband, Pierre, and their friends. They all conspired to acquire two airline tickets just a few days before they were needed. God had used so many people to help us over those five months. We had an opportunity to see a few folks from our church school family who came to our house to visit. We anticipated seeing even more at Easter Mass.

Everyone who saw Joshua was amazed at how good he looked. I hoped it would make them feel good that they had been a part of his miracle. Few people get to experience that in a lifetime. We prayed that part of the ripple effect of this miracle was that everyone who played any part in it would get to experience a deeper understanding of the power of faith, and how God works through us as long as we are open to it.

It is so wonderful to share in such incredible joy through your sharing with us! Thank you Dave, Gwen, and Josh for your Trust in Jesus to pull you through such an incredible journey. I know there is still more yet to walk, but with eyes opened wide there is definitely a Light that shows you the way!

—*Kathy Wendel*

Wow what a very beautiful and powerful testimony of God's grace and love. Happy Easter to you all! Because He lives!

—*mindy gibbons*

Loved seeing you at the airport. I felt like I hugged a miracle!!!

—*Melody Reed*

I'm way behind on my reading. God has perfect timing. Today is the day I needed to read this. God bless you all as your miracles continue to bless others and give them hope. Love and hugs, Paula

—*Paula Findley*

• — •

The last weeks in Houston were bittersweet. Arrangements had to be made, and final goodbyes had to be said. There were so many people to thank, from doctors, nurses, and therapists to apartment managers, the staff at Walgreens, and new friends. While Gwen and Joshua had never wanted to be there as long as they had, they had developed friendships with therapists, nurses and, of course, the Davises.

Gwen and Joshua, with Robin's help, were able to make return visits to TIRR and Memorial Hermann to say "thank you" to the doctors, staff, and nurses who cared for him. They were so appreciative that Joshua came to visit. They had seen him at his worst, and we did not want those memories to be the ones they carried with them. All of the nurses we engaged said that return visits like this were incredibly rare and that it helped them remember that their work makes a positive difference in people's lives. They told us that these are the memories that help get them through days of cranky patients, double shifts, more patients than they can handle, and deaths. These visits were also a promise fulfilled that "Joshua and I will walk back in here someday and give you a proper hug."

Kristi recalled that "Josh and Gwen came by the hospital prior to leaving. I walked out to say goodbye, and I just couldn't help it, I cried.

I'm not a crier, but I sobbed like a baby. I sobbed with Mom when I saw the relief on her face as it was finally over, and with Sugarplum thinking of everything he'd accomplished, and for myself because they were really leaving me. Patients come and go, but this was different. This was personal. Knowing that Josh was going home soon, like home-home, walking on his own two feet, was, and is, by far the single most memorable moment of my career."

It was time to go home.

Homecoming

Joshua and Gwen came home for good on May 13, 2018. A Sunday. Mother's Day.

How appropriate that our family was reunited on the day set aside as a tribute to our mothers, even though on this particular day, Gwen was traveling. She missed out on all the typical Mother's Day festivities—family gatherings, presents, a nice meal in a restaurant. She didn't care. She was exactly where she wanted to be … bringing her son home.

While Joshua's recovery was far from complete, this was yet another major milestone. Our son was alive, and we were back together. He still had an eye surgery in his future, but he could walk, talk, and think. For all of us, and especially for Gwen, this was the best Mother's Day ever.

After my vision of Joshua's recovery, we had continued to pay rent and utilities on his apartment in anticipation of his return. Most folks would have questioned that decision in November and December, when Joshua was mostly unconscious, barely responsive, fed through a tube, on a ventilator, with a quarter of his skull missing. It was also a questionable decision when, in the months to follow, he was barely able to walk, couldn't speak, had a trach tube, and couldn't remember what happened five minutes earlier. Fortunately, we ignored all that because we truly believed that God had a plan, and we trusted that plan.

Was it the right financial decision? Absolutely not! Were we blind to the odds of his survival and ability to ever lead a normal life? You bet! God was in charge. It wasn't our plan. We had to let it play out. No matter where it led, we believed we would all have what we needed when we needed it.

After Joshua and Gwen returned home, we entered the next phase of recovery. Joshua wanted to move back into his apartment immediately. Shocker! He was twenty-one and wanted his life back. Not surprising. Gwen and I decided that it would be best if he stayed with us for a bit. We didn't know what "a bit" meant, but we felt we needed to keep him under observation as he acclimated to this new normal. While Joshua was supremely confident, at this point we weren't sure if he could manage all the tasks of independent daily living.

In the weeks that passed Joshua continued to improve. He had gradually gained back the thirty pounds he had lost and added fifteen more. He looked strong and healthy now. His latest eye exam revealed that he had 20/20 vision, although his left eye was not properly aligned, causing his vision to be double and blurry at times. He was still wearing an eye patch. Although he still moved slowly and cautiously at times, he jogged when we went to the gym. His voice sounded a bit different than before the accident, and his speech was sometimes a bit off. Short-term memory was still a challenge, but he used technology—of course he did—to remind himself about tasks and deadlines. All in all, his recovery had been nothing short of miraculous and we all felt very blessed.

After a few weeks at our house, Joshua moved back into his apartment. The apartment was fifteen minutes away from our house. Joshua couldn't drive initially because someone had wrapped his car around a tree back in November, so we picked him up and took him places. He had to make lists and set reminders for most everything, could be easily distracted, and was often fatigued after a few hours of focused effort. It was amazing to me that he could remember the shirt he wore in his first-grade school picture but not what he had for breakfast that morning. As we learned, all of this was common with TBI. While he looked fine and communicated well, we were told it would take several more years for him to reach his full recovery. TBI can truly be an invisible injury.

Joshua had been working on an app for the owner of a large local roofing company at the time of his accident. He had completed Phase One of the app, and Joel, the owner, waited on him to return and finish the project. What an act of kindness and trust! Joshua was able to resume work on the app and generate income.

Only time would tell if he was ready to resume his career as a young entrepreneur. During this period Gwen and I commented to each other that Joshua laughed more than he ever had. We had read and heard that some TBI survivors can experience personality changes that cause them to be bitter, hateful, and even violent. We were thankful that this was not the case with our son. There had been times before the accident when he could be selfish and a bit arrogant. Now, he seemed more joyous, thankful, and sensitive. I talked about these differences with Joshua; we were both prone to analyze and compare things. Despite his current challenges with memory and focus, he felt he was a better person after the accident.

Joshua had what we hoped would be one last surgical procedure on his trachea scheduled soon. It was another in a series of procedures to remove scar tissue from his trachea to keep it open. We planned to return to Houston for a few days for that surgery and hopefully see our dear friends, the Davises, who had been so supportive and helpful. God blessed us in a mighty way by placing them in our path.

Joshua had always been obsessed with cars. That had not changed. He had done a good job of saving his earnings prior to the accident, and now that he was back to working with income coming in, he was prepared to buy his next car. While Gwen and I certainly suffered financially through all this, we had been able to protect his savings. He had saved enough to make a significant down payment on an older Porsche 987. Was it practical? No, but he did his homework and paid a reasonable price. Was it the car his mother would have preferred he bought? No, she preferred a tank or some sort of armored vehicle with a top speed of thirty miles per hour. For Joshua, though, driving had always been not just fun but therapeutic. Sometimes, to get his mind right for the day ahead, or when he was feeling fatigued after a few hours of focused work, he'd take a short drive. He said it helped clear his head and gave him some time for brainstorming. Some of his best business ideas were produced on these drives.

The transition back home had been great, but also challenging, especially for Gwen. She had been Joshua's constant caregiver for many months, and the stress of that responsibility had taken a toll on her. In addition, she had seen and experienced some traumatic things that could not be unseen or blocked out. At some point, she was going to have to deal with that. In a sense, she was also recovering and reconnecting with our family and friends and her school and church family. The Immaculate Conception School family was amazing, offering constant prayer, continued paychecks, videos of her class, and meals and rides for me.

This is a portion of my CaringBridge post in early June:

> My wife is a ROCK! She was faced with a challenging, emotional, gut wrenching situation and, with God's help, handled it with grace and patience. I am thoroughly convinced that God placed her, rather than me, in that caregiver role. He knew that only the persistence and patience of a loving mother could get Joshua through this. She was afraid for Joshua's life many times, but willed herself through it in order to make major decisions regarding his care. As she has said, "It has been very hard at times but I wouldn't be anywhere else." We just celebrated our 35th wedding anniversary and I love her more, admire her more, and appreciate her more now than I ever have. She is the greatest blessing of my life.

Joshua's close friends had also been great. Although communication had been limited for many months, they went out of their way to include him in activities once he had returned home. He was truly blessed to have good friends like Brandon, Seth, and Bryce. Those four young men had been friends and schoolmates most of their lives.

In the early days of our transition to a more normal life, I observed that there were challenges ahead for all of us. For months, we'd been in the cocoon of survival and recovery. It was an isolated environment where we were totally focused on staying strong in our faith, dealing with Joshua's current medical challenge, and keeping each other strong. Yes, I was back to work, and it was a distraction from our situation at times, but when I wasn't completing a task I was in the cocoon. In the cocoon, we didn't care about social media, what was on television, the stock market, planning our next vacation, or the neighborhood gossip. Now that we were all back home, we were back in the world—the world where we get pulled in every direction on a daily basis, where we can be bombarded with information, most of which is meaningless. Where the daily to-do list is seldom completed and keeps getting longer. In our Christian faith Jesus calls us to be "in the world" but not "of the world." It was obvious to me that now we were back in the world, and it was going to be a challenge to stay focused on our faith, our thankfulness, and paying it forward.

While we were transitioning back to our normal life, it was time to begin the "Thank You" tour and attempt to visit with as many of Joshua's caregivers and supporters as possible. We had a ton of giving back and paying forward to do. From the nurses and doctors at UAMS to Father West's congregation in Texarkana, we had many people to thank. The Hispanic families in Father West's congregation had sold their homemade food to raise $700, which they donated to us. It was wonderful to see

Father Joseph at Mass. He had comforted Gwen and me and prayed over Joshua several times, as had our dear friend Father West. While there were still many medical bills and other expenses to pay, we were also most appreciative to all our donors, especially Miracles for Mary. While not one of these supporters expected to be recognized or repaid, we felt duty-bound to at least tell them "thank you" and pay it forward as best we could.

It should not have been a surprise that our first Mass together after Gwen and Joshua returned home for good was a special one. In the rush to get ready and be on time, none of us had noticed that this particular Mass was in celebration of Pentecost. Pentecost is celebrated ten days after Ascension Thursday, in observance of Jesus' ascension into Heaven, and commemorates the descent of the Holy Spirit upon the Apostles and other followers of Jesus Christ while they were in Jerusalem.

When Father John told the congregation that we were celebrating Pentecost—a time of new beginning, as he described it—Gwen and I looked at one another, smiled, and held hands. *Of course it was*, we thought. Like many things along our journey, particular people and elements of our faith had supported us at just the right time, or confirmed that we were on the right path. I had posted many months earlier about "God Things and Blessings," and those elements of our journey were tangible and undeniable. The fact that our first Mass together since Gwen and Joshua returned home was a celebration of new beginnings was yet another in a string of such events. God had always given us what we needed when we needed it. The knowledge and trust that it would always be that way gave us hope and helped us to be unafraid.

I began to understand that we all have to look for those signs in our lives. Sometimes we must look deeply to see through the fog and chaos of everyday life. I promise you, the signs of our many blessings are there. They are always there. When you see them, cherish them, say a prayer of thanks, and keep looking.

It was pure joy to see Josh and Gwen at school a couple weeks ago. I'm so excited they are home and continuing to recover!!! Prayers have been answered, and miracles have occurred!! God is good! Just let me know if I can do ANYTHING!

—Alyssa Matthews

God is good! I love to read how He continues to bless you in this journey!

—Gigi Parker

Coincidences are only the whispers of the Holy Spirit. You were all meant to be there for a reason. How beautiful was God's timing. We saw Fr. Chan recently at one of the ordinations at Christ the King. Josh and your family were in our conversations and prayers that day. Thx for sharing your post. Paul.

—Paul Wendel

You are so right, David. I am about to celebrate my 87th birthday, and my numerous experiences have revealed God's goodness time after time. Nothing is so valuable as a strong faith.

—Ruth Roberts

Do you recall the promise I made early on in this journey? If not, let me remind you. It took more than a week after my admission to UAMS to get through pelvis surgery, be discharged, and get to Joshua's room. When I arrived in his room Joshua had undergone life-saving surgery just a few days earlier to remove his skull flaps and release the pressure on his swelling brain. He was unconscious, immobile, with a feeding tube, breathing tube, a dozen or more medications hung from metal stands, and tubes and wires were running everywhere. Even with all of this medical intervention, Joshua's temperature and heart rate often rose to dangerous levels for long periods of time due to the inability of his brain to control his body.

Despite this desperate situation, divine intervention gave me a different vision. My vision was that Joshua and God were working on the greatest rewiring project of all time, that Joshua was untangling the mess of wires in his brain as he had done with so many of his projects, and that God was guiding his hands, reassuring him, and helping him to be patient and keep trying.

That vision gave me comfort. I knew in my heart that Joshua would be okay eventually. Knowing that these nurses were working hard to keep him alive, and that, as they had told us, they seldom knew if patients fully recovered once they left the ICU, I made a promise to the doctors and nurses that cared for Joshua.

The promise was simply this: "Joshua and I will walk back in here someday and give you all a proper hug." It was a pretty bold promise considering Joshua's situation, and mine, at the time. Joshua and Gwen had already fulfilled that promise with the doctors and nurses at TIRR in Houston. Now, the fulfillment of that promise began at UAMS. God is good, His power is infinite, and with Him all things are possible.

That evening in mid-June was filled with hugs, laughter, and a few tears. Gwen, Joshua, and I spent several hours visiting with the nurses and doctors who cared for him during his weeks in ICU and on the trauma ward. For Joshua, it was an introduction to the people who kept him alive and cared for him 24/7. He had not been fully conscious and didn't remember any of the caregivers or visitors except for a few voices. He had to feel a bit awkward, but he took it all in stride and thanked them all with a proper hug.

Comments from my CaringBridge post:

I remember you telling me that promise of you and Joshua from your wheelchair in the hospital. I believed it then. Your words, strength, and faith as well as Gwen's kept my hope alive as I watched you as a family. I will never forget those days at the hospital. I am changed forever.

—*Melody Reed*

I have tears in my eyes as I read your post. I remember praying for you and Josh as those first days unfolded. I also remember the words of Monsignor Friend that echoed in my head as I prayed, that "all prayers must be accompanied with the full confidence and expectation that they will be fully answered if they are in accordance with God's will". This is a fulfillment of those prayers and gives me further proof that God is good all the time and if we have the faith to surrender to that will, all will be good too.

I suspect that this journey will fulfill many other private promises you made with our good Lord. I bet there will be a family one day in an ICU whose loved one has just suffered a TBI, that you will love and support and be their rock . I love you brother. Your faith and perseverance in this chapter of your life is inspiring. Paul

—*Paul Wendel*

Dear Moody family,

Our families have never met but we have traveled a similar path. We join you in praising God for healing our sons!

To God be Glory forever and ever!

Dan and Gigi Parker Parents of Lee Parker (Caring-Bridge - leeparker3)

—*Gigi Parker*

Sydney, one of Joshua's nurses at UAMS, recalls, "The day that Joshua walked back onto the unit was one that I definitely will not forget. It's one of those experiences that you think about after horrible shifts where you wonder why you became a nurse in the first place. Joshua is my why. He's that one that defied all odds and medical diagnoses and showed me there is always room to have faith in patients when medicine tells you not to.

"I'm still amazed by his recovery. It's a story I still tell, all my family and close friends feel like they know Joshua on a first-name basis because he's the miracle I've talked about the most in my nursing career. It is pretty amazing that I got to begin my nursing career with a real-life walking, talking miracle."

Despite the dire situation, I always felt Joshua would recover. I can only attribute that to accepting that The Almighty had us in his arms and that, no matter the outcome, He would give us all what we needed to get through it. A big part of what He gave us was highly skilled, caring nurses and doctors, some of whom had become dear friends. They not only cared for Joshua, but they let us share our fears and concerns with them and consoled us at times. I believe they recognized that we were a close-knit, loving, faith-filled family with friends who would be with us 24/7 throughout Joshua's stay. They responded accordingly by accommodating the frequent visitors, working around our luggage and daily living supplies scattered about the room, answering a barrage of questions, and patiently listening when we needed to talk. We have great respect and love for Joshua's nurses and doctors. We owe them his life, and we will spend the rest of our lives trying to pay it back and pay it forward.

Joshua was scheduled for one more throat surgery. We hoped that this bronchoscopy in Houston would be the last one. It was his fifth surgery to clear away scar tissue that could impede airflow in his trachea and over his vocal cords. We prayed once more that God's healing hand would be on Joshua and also with his doctors and nurses.

On this return trip to Houston, we had the opportunity to thank a few more folks who had been so helpful while Gwen and Joshua were there. Although it didn't work out, we had hoped to meet the Tullier family who helped us decide to send Joshua to TIRR. We visited with the Davis family who had been so good to us. They have truly been a blessing and are now our dear friends.

As for me, I recovered just fine with no complications or persistent pain, except when I tried to do too much. About ten months after the accident, I attended a high school reunion. Many of my classmates knew about the accident. White Hall High was a small school when I graduated, and a number of us have stayed connected through the years. I was talking with a group of guys that I played sports with all through school when someone asked how I was doing. I replied that I was recovering well, that I was back in the gym and walking for exercise routinely—but I still couldn't run. Almost in unison they replied, "Moody, you never *could* run!" So there you have it. I had achieved total recovery and didn't realize it.

Joshua eventually met with Dr. Paula Grigorian, an eye surgeon at UAMS, and the surgery to correct his strabismus was successful. His eye was very red for a few weeks, as expected. He'd had double vision and blurry vision over the past months. Now it was back to 20/20 and clear. He told me he was most thankful that he no longer saw two of me. "One is more than enough," he said.

So, this portion of our journey had come to a close. In an instant, Joshua lost everything—his business, his car, and nearly his life. From unconscious and immobile just months earlier, he had regained his ability to see, move, eat, speak, and think. He was more joyous and sensitive to others. His faith was stronger. Although he could easily have been bitter and angry with me for driving him into a tree, he wasn't. In fact, he always considered it just an accident that could have happened to anyone.

Gwen's ability to dream gradually returned once she was back home. She had been protected for the past six months from reliving all the trauma she had experienced while she slept. I'm still amazed by this. The downside was that I could again be in trouble in the early morning hours after something I allegedly did in her dreams. I didn't mind at all.

God put some wonderful people in our path along the journey, and I was sure there were more to come. I'm never quite sure whether people were put in our path so they could help us or for us to help them. I tried to not overthink it and just let God handle the trip planning. I sure did feel like we'd been the recipients of the help far more often than we had contributed. I knew our turn was coming, though; in fact, it had already started. We felt that and welcomed it. I often think that I am a simple piece of conduit. My job is to let God's love flow through me and not get in the way. As my marketing friends say, "Don't step on the message."

We know we have not been through this experience to keep what we learned to ourselves. We were, and still are, fully committed to helping any families we can through this TBI journey. We had already started doing that as people reached out to us with their stories. Our friend Nancy is at Arkansas Children's Hospital. She posted this note on CaringBridge.

> David, the family that I introduced you to is now at TIRR, as of last week. I know that your visit was a big influence in their decision. Prayers for Joshua and all involved on Monday as well as you and Gwen. Thank you for your ongoing commitment. Nancy Thomas
>
> —*Nancy Thomas, June 23, 2018*

And so, as the journey of TBI survival and recovery begins for another family, we are working hard to continue to be thankful, let God lead the way, and pay it forward as best we can.

Medical Biographies

PAULA GRIGORIAN, MD, is an Associate Professor of Ophthalmology and a pediatric ophthalmologist. She received her medical degree from the University of Medicine and Pharmacy Carol Davila in Bucharest, Romania. She completed her surgical internship and ophthalmic residency in Romania and an additional ophthalmology residency at UAMS. She went on to complete a fellowship in pediatric ophthalmology at the University of Texas Southwestern in Dallas. Her clinical expertise includes adults and kids with strabismus, children with cataracts, genetic eye conditions, neuro-ophthalmology conditions, and retinopathy of prematurity.

SHAWN S. GROTH, MD, is a general thoracic surgeon specializing in minimally invasive esophageal surgery. After finishing his cardiothoracic surgery residency at the Harvard Medical School's Brigham and Women's Hospital, Dr. Groth pursued an advanced fellowship in minimally invasive esophageal surgery at the University of Pittsburgh under the mentorship of Dr. James D. Luketich, a pioneer in minimally invasive foregut surgery.

DR. MARY KATHERINE KIMBROUGH, MD, is a physician and Assistant Professor in the Division of Trauma and Critical Care Surgery at UAMS Medical Center. Dr. Kimbrough earned her bachelor's degree at Louisiana Tech University and her medical degree and residency at Louisiana State University Medical School at Shreveport. Dr. Kimbrough completed a trauma/surgical critical care fellowship at Louisiana State University at New Orleans. Dr. Kimbrough is board certified by the American Board of Surgery in General Surgery and Surgical Critical Care Surgery. She is also an Advanced Trauma Life Support (ATLS) Certified Instructor. Dr. Kimbrough is an Associate Fellow member in the American College of Surgeons and a member of the Alpha Omega Alpha Medical Honor Society.

DR. RYAN KITAGAWA came to Memorial Hermann–Texas Medical Center and University of Texas Health from the University of Miami Miller School of Medicine, where he served as a research fellow and completed his neurosurgery fellowship. He is a graduate of Northwestern University and received his medical degree and neurosurgery training at the Baylor College of Medicine in Houston. He also served on several research teams at the University of Texas M.D. Anderson Cancer Center and Northwestern University's Department of Biomedical Engineering.

DR. RONALD D. ROBERTSON is a physician and professor in the Department of Surgery at UAMS Medical Center. He received his bachelor's degree at the University of Arkansas at Fayetteville and his medical degree from UAMS. His post-graduate education includes a fellowship in the Trauma & Critical Care unit at UAMS Medical Center. He is currently the medical director of the Advanced Trauma Life Support (ATLS) course sponsored by the UAMS Department of Surgery and the American College of Surgeons.

Dr. Robertson is board-eligible for the American College of Surgeons and was the recipient of the Robert M. Bransford, MD Memorial Award for Outstanding Chief Resident in General Surgery in 1995 as well as the Society of Laparoendoscopic Surgeons Resident Achievement Award winner in 1994. At UAMS, Dr. Robertson serves on the Academic Affairs Committee and the Multidisciplinary Committee on Pain Management.

He is also a member of the Arkansas Medical Society, the American College of Surgeons, and the Society of Laparoendoscopic Surgeons.

DR. ANALIZ RODRIGUEZ MD, PHD, attended New College of Florida, the honors college of Florida's state university system, majoring in chemistry. She then attended the National Institutes of Health-sponsored Medical Scientist Training Program at Case Western Reserve University, obtaining both her MD. and PhD. Dr. Rodriguez completed her neurosurgical residency at Wake Forest University Medical Center. She completed her neurosurgical oncology fellowship at City of Hope National Medical Center which specializes in immunotherapy clinical trials.

During her neurosurgical training, Dr. Rodriguez earned numerous awards and honors such as a Neurosurgery Research Education Foundation Research Fellowship, CNS Leadership Fellowship, and CSNS Socioeconomic Fellowship. Dr. Rodriguez's main research interests include the use of laser thermal ablation for brain tumors and understanding the immune microenvironment. She is a member of the Clinician Scientist Program at UAMS.

About the Author

David Moody is the founder of business consulting firm Jacksson David LLC, former Deputy Director of the U.S. Small Business Administration Arkansas District Office, and a NASA guy. He served for thirteen years in the aerospace industry as a program analyst, manager, and consultant for the Shuttle, Space Lab, and Space Station programs.

David has owned and operated several businesses in the fields of risk management, retail and business consulting, run a $52 million program for the Arkansas Energy Office, and invested in dozens of Arkansas startup companies. His consulting firm provides a variety of services for small and medium-sized businesses. He was recently named as the Executive Director for the Ark Angel Alliance and leads the Minority Business Empowerment Fund program with Southern Bancorp and the Croom Firm. His newest endeavor is developing the Faith-Based Executive Officers (FBXO) peer group.

David has served on a variety of boards including nonprofits dedicated to education, technology training, veterans, and supporting startup companies. In addition to consulting, David also enjoys speaking and writing on leadership, organizational culture, and entrepreneurship and has a social media following as StartupDad.

David is a devoted husband, father, grandfather, and Christian. He enjoys the outdoors, skiing, sports, and playing the drums.

Printed in the USA
CPSIA information can be obtained
at www.ICGtesting.com
CBHW051757280924
15003CB00004B/12